HOW TO HEAR GOD: ACTIVATION GUIDE

How to Hear God: Activation Guide

Copyright © 2020 Sterling Harris

ISBN: 978-1-7353469-2-2

All rights reserved. No part of this book may be used or reproduced by any means, graphic, electronic, mechanical, including photocopying, recording, taping, or by any information storage retrieval system without the written permission of the author except in the case of brief quotations embodied in critical articles and reviews.

Scriptures taken from the Holy Bible, New International Version®, NIV®. Copyright © 1973, 1978, 1984, 2011 by Biblica, Inc.™ Used by permission of Zondervan. All rights reserved worldwide. www.zondervan.com The "NIV" and "New International Version" are trademarks registered in the United States Patent and Trademark Office by Biblica, Inc.™ | The Holy Bible, English Standard Version® (ESV®) Copyright © 2001 by Crossway, a publishing ministry of Good News Publishers. All rights reserved. | Scripture taken from the New King James Version®. Copyright © 1982 by Thomas Nelson. Used by permission. All rights reserved. | Scripture quotations marked MSG are taken from THE MESSAGE, copyright © 1993, 1994, 1995, 1996, 2000, 2001, 2002 by Eugene H. Peterson. Used by permission of NavPress. All rights reserved. Represented by Tyndale House Publishers, Inc. | Scripture taken from the Amplified Bible, Copyright © 1954, 1958, 1962, 1964, 1965, 1987 by The Lockman Foundation. Used by permission. | Scripture quotations marked TPT are from The Passion Translation®. Copyright © 2017, 2018 by Passion & Fire Ministries, Inc. Used by permission. All rights reserved. ThePassionTranslation.com. | Scripture quotations from The Authorized (King James) Version. Rights in the Authorized Version in the United Kingdom are vested in the Crown. Reproduced by permission of the Crown's patentee, Cambridge University Press | Scriptures marked as "(GNT)" are taken from the **Good News Translation - Second Edition** © 1992 by American Bible Society. Used by permission. | Scripture quoted by permission. Quotations designated (NET) are from the NET Bible® copyright ©1996, 2019 by Biblical Studies Press, L.L.C. http://netbible.com All rights reserved| Scripture quotations marked PARA are paraphrasing of the original text by the author.

Assistant Project Editors:

Dr. Peter Running | Leah Harris

HOW TO HEAR GOD: ACTIVATION GUIDE

10 Ways God Speaks

STERLING HARRIS

Tall Pine

Contents

HOW TO USE THIS GUIDE	v
1. THE JOURNEY AND THE QUEST BEGIN	1
2. GOD'S WORD	9
3. PRAYER (PART 1)	17
4. PRAYER (PART 2)	25
5. THE HOLY SPIRIT	35
6. THE INWARD WITNESS	47
7. CIRCUMSTANCES	55
8. THE CHURCH AND OTHER PEOPLE	63
9. DREAMS AND VISIONS	71
10. CHRISTIAN MUSIC AND WORSHIP	79
11. CREATION	87
12. THE DEMONSTRATION OF GOD'S LOVE AND POWER (PART 1)	95
13. THE DEMONSTRATION OF GOD'S LOVE AND POWER (PART 2)	103
14. SPREADING GOD'S LOVE AND PARTNERSHIP	117
GIVING	119
AUTHOR BIO	121

HOW TO USE THIS GUIDE
SUGGESTIONS FROM THE AUTHOR

Suggestions to get the most out of this workbook and activation guide for individual study:

- Take the time to read the text and even write notes in the margins of things that seem to touch your heart.
- Non-Negotiables: These are the main truths and takeaways from the section.
- Reflection Questions: These are designed to be answered according to your heart's intent on hearing God's perspective on the questions, as well as your own. Intentionally partnering with God for the answers is the aim. For this reason, we have added the phrase "Pray, Ask and Listen:" to some of the questions as a reminder to partner with God on the answers. For your convenience, we reference the page numbers of the book that inspired the reflection questions.

HOW TO USE THIS GUIDE

- Activation Decree: This is you taking authority over your life and partnering with God for breakthrough, change and transformation. Your spoken words have POWER, so please say this decree out loud, in faith, like you want it to come to pass in your life!
- Setting Expectations: These are action steps, mindsets and goals for you to continue in and to apply them to your daily life. This will ensure long-lasting peace, freedom and love.
- At the end of each chapter, we encourage you to write down further goals and expectations, as well as God experiences and encounters that relate to that specific chapter.

Suggestions to get the most out of this workbook and activation guide in a group setting:

- Read the text aloud as a group, taking turns, allowing one person to read at a time. This helps to keep everyone engaged.
- As people are reading, there will often be talking points within the reading that you can use to generate conversation. Make sure you take the time to stop when you sense God is prompting the group to discuss something within the reading and interact with the group. This is meant to be an interactive workbook and activation guide.
- Non-Negotiables: These are the main truths and takeaways from the section.
- Reflection Questions: These are designed to be answered according to your heart's intent on hearing

God's perspective on the questions, as well as your own. Intentionally partnering with God for the answers is the aim. For this reason, we have added the phrase "Pray, Ask and Listen:" to some of the questions as a reminder to partner with God on the answers. For your convenience, we reference the page numbers of the book that inspired the reflection questions.
- Encourage people within the group to share God stories and personal encounters that tie into the Reflection Questions.
- Activation Decree: This is about the group taking authority over their lives and partnering with God for breakthrough, change and transformation. Your spoken words have POWER, so please have the whole group read this decree out loud together, in faith, like you all want it to come to pass in your life and in the lives of all the group members!
- Setting Expectations: These are action steps, mindsets and goals for each person to continue in. This will ensure long-lasting peace, freedom and love within their daily lives.
- At the end of each chapter, we encourage everyone to write down further goals and expectations, as well as God experiences and encounters that relate to that specific chapter.

1

THE JOURNEY AND THE QUEST BEGIN
CHAPTER ONE ACTIVATION GUIDE

SETTING THE STAGE

God's voice is not the finish line but the starting line. His voice is not an *end* in itself but a means to an end—and that *end* is a deep, vibrant, and intimate relationship with Jesus Christ. As we kick start this journey and tackle the diverse topics related to God's voice, it's important to recognize that all of these topics are meant to funnel us to one single point: a love-relationship with God. Intimacy with God is the lifelong process of experiencing Him in all of His ways, and understanding His love, character, nature and Word. It's a two-way street of communication from the depths of your heart to the depths of His, and then back again. Hearing from God is not merely a *bonus* of a relationship with Him but the *foundation* of a relationship with Him.

Think of it, when you gave your life to Jesus, you made that choice *under the influence*. Who's influence? *God's influence!* He drew us to Himself at salvation. Jesus said, "No one can come to me unless the Father who sent me draws them, and I will raise them up on the last day" (John 6:44 NIV). Thus, if you have been saved, you have heard from God. You have responded to His leading. Yet it does not stop there. We now have the honor of fine-tuning our senses and growing in our grasp of the many ways in which God speaks. The methods by which He speaks vary, yet His motivation stays the same—*love*. God loves you!—and He *likes* you! You are in His *inner circle*.

Many of us battle a sense of deep rejection due to things like childhood trauma or past failures. As a result, we struggle to believe that we're accepted by God, let alone believe that we are part of God's "inner circle" of communication. Yet, the blood of Christ Jesus was shed at Calvary in order to forgive your offenses and clear your tainted record. In God's eyes, you are as spotless as His Son, Jesus. You might ponder what this has to do with hearing from God. Look at it this way, God's voice is looking for a *runway*, and the runway He is looking for is a person who believes the right things about Him, and believes the right things about himself or herself. The belief of our heart can indeed beckon us to seek God's voice.

Without salvation and a clear belief about the nature of God, our hearts will lack the preparedness we need to receive the fullness of God's voice. God might still speak to us, yet we will be on the wrong frequency and may miss it! If you're reading this workbook and you've never received Jesus as your personal Lord and Savior, I encourage you to pause now and read pages 5-8 in *How to Hear God*. This will provide the necessary platform upon which the rest of your life may be assembled.

Some say, "Life is short," yet, in reality, for the believer, life is eternal. (See John 11:26.) If we are going about an *eternal* adventure, we ought to have a roadmap or navigation system to help us find the best path. Are you the type of person who is all about the destination or the journey? What if I told you, you can be *both*?

As Christians, we are all about our heavenly destination. Yet, at the same time, we have a purpose on earth that we must walk out properly, and doing so without proper *navigational instruments* would be costly. The voice of God is our GPS along the way. GPS stands for *Global Positioning System*. The job of this device is to tell us *where we are* and *where we are going*. Likewise, the Holy Spirit locates us right where we are and then leads us to where He is calling us, step by step.

Have you ever found yourself driving, enjoying music, when the GPS interrupts the song to give directions? It lowers the volume of the other voice in order to emphasize and make clear the directions it's giving. In our lives, many voices are present and fighting for our focus. The goal of this section of the book is to lower the volume of competing voices in order to set the stage for God's voice to be heard. As with any skill, hearing God can be learned and refined. We don't start as experts in *anything*, and spiritual matters are not exempt from that reality. As we go about exploring the *methods* by which God speaks, it's important that our leadings pass this quick reliability test. Ask yourself:

- Does what I sense, see and/or hear agree with the Bible and the *loving* nature of God?
- Does this inner voice flow from a place of peace, love, hope and wisdom?
- Does this voice produce the *fruit of the Spirit* as defined in Galatians 5:22-23?
- Does what I am experiencing lead to fear, anxiety,

shame, unworthiness or other things that don't resemble Jesus?

This simple test will enable you to discern and decipher if you're experiencing the voice of God. You may not always be completely certain, and that's okay. We are all in the process of learning and stepping out in faith. Faith is a muscle—it requires action to grow. In the same way that a bodybuilder cannot compete because he did one workout, we, as believers, cannot maximize our lives by hearing God *occasionally*. It must be *daily!*

You may find that as you look back at your life, God was speaking clearly—you just didn't pick up on the signal. I can certainly recall times when God was communicating clearly with me but I simply overlooked it. This is avoidable as we recognize the *methods* and *motivations* behind the voice of God and position ourselves to pick up the signal that heaven is releasing.

THE **NON-NEGOTIABLES**

- *Intimacy* with God is the goal of *communication* with God.
- You are *forgiven* and *free*. God loves you, likes you and you're worthy of His voice and blessing.
- God has given us parameters in His Word to help us identify when He speaks.
- Hearing God's voice daily is not merely *possible* but *necessary*.

REFLECTION QUESTIONS

Things like guilt, shame, condemnation and unworthiness cause *static* in our ability to hear God. (See page 3.) Take some time to pray and listen. Jesus, what are some areas in my heart that are hindering me from hearing Your voice with greater clarity that You want to remove? If God highlights things that need to be dealt with in your heart, talk them over with God; repent and give those things over to Him. Make note of the experience below:

_____
_____
_____
_____
_____
_____

Walking with Jesus means allowing the Holy Spirit to guide your thoughts, words and actions. (See page 4.) How does this direction from God's voice currently impact your life, practically speaking? How would allowing Him to guide you impact your world in the next months, years and decades?

_____
_____
_____
_____
_____
_____

Looking back, do you recognize times when God was speaking but you weren't listening? How can you avoid neglecting His voice as you move forward? (See page 9.) Write out your plan to hear from the Holy Spirit on a daily basis:

_____
_____
_____
_____
_____
_____

ACTIVATION DECREE

I decree and declare that I am now activated with an appetite to receive and experience the voice of God in my daily life. With a clear heart and greater clarity and receptivity than ever, I will go forth with eyes to see and ears to hear precisely what the Spirit of the Lord is saying to me! In Jesus Name Amen!

SETTING **EXPECTATIONS**

In the days, weeks and months to come, you should:

- Keep and maintain a clear heart, free from the things Jesus died to remove.
- Recognize that God *actually* enjoys speaking to you and wants to do so.
- Study the biblical parameters God has set up for His voice in your life.
- Journal your experiences as you step out in hearing the voice of God.

Feel free to write out further goals, expectations and God experiences in the space below:

_____
_____
_____
_____
_____
_____
_____

STERLING HARRIS

> 2
>
> # GOD'S WORD
> CHAPTER TWO ACTIVATION GUIDE

THE WRITTEN VOICE OF GOD

The Word of God is the unadulterated *will of God.* If you want to understand God's heart and God's desires, look no further than the Bible itself. The truth of the Word has no expiration date—it's not merely a historical document but a *living voice.* For so long, I viewed the Bible as a list of rules. I considered it to be a harsh text, highlighting my sins and bad choices. I saw God as a Taskmaster who was ready to zap me for not getting my act together! Yet after I began know God relationally instead of out my prior religious duty and I started reading the Bible for myself with a new filter of His goodness and love I had personally experienced, my view shifted and I no longer saw the Bible as a rule book but as a love letter to me.

I now see God's love for me clearly in the Bible as He lays out who I am and how He feels about me. Not only that, but when the Scriptures command me to do something or to *not* do something, I see God's love in that also! For example, let's say you have an eight-year-old son and you tell him, "Don't touch this stove. It is hot and will burn you and cause you pain." If he did touch it and burned himself, or didn't follow the rules, would you love him any less? The answer is no! Beyond that, was your instruction harsh or overbearing? Of course not! You simply wanted to prevent his pain. Likewise, God provides guidance, boundaries, instruction and encouragement from His Word that will prevent unnecessary pain in our lives and set us up for success.

In the same way that there is a *right* way and a *wrong* way to drive a car, there is a right way and a wrong way to study the Bible. Paul urges us in Scripture to "rightly divide the Word of God." (See 2 Timothy 2:15.) He gave this instruction because many in his day (and in our day) *wrongly* divide the Word of God. The Bible is unlike any other book and must be studied unlike any other book. Here are a few pointers for interpreting the Bible correctly and getting the most out of the experience. As you read it, ask:

1. What did the passage I just read mean to the people in the time in which it was written?
2. What does the passage I just read mean to us now, and how does it apply to our lives today?
3. What does this passage mean to me personally, and how can I currently apply this to my life?

These clarifying questions will improve your experience in the Word greatly. Not only that, but more importantly, the Bible is meant to be read in *cooperation* with the Holy Spirit. The Holy Spirit inspired the words of the Bible, and it's the Holy Spirit who provides us with its interpretation. Many non-believers, atheists and agnostics have read the Bible and not received anything from it. Why? Because the Scriptures are meant to be received by faith and with a heart that is in sync with the Holy Spirit. In this place, His Word will come alive and you will see it in a new way.

When the Bible came alive to me, I began to notice that in my daily devotions, a passage of Scripture would speak to me about exactly what I was going through at that time. God was communicating to me through His Word, right where I was. It began to transform my mind and feed my spirit. As the seed of the Word was planted in me, I noticed that I had some "de-weeding" to do. We must tend the garden of our hearts to weed out fear, doubt, shame, worry, unworthiness, offense, irritation and frustration.

The Devil knows that *you + the Word of God = dangerous*. As a result, he does all he can to intercept the Word from getting to you. As you begin experiencing God's voice through the Bible, you might find that strange thoughts, doubts and distractions come to the surface. You must put out these fires with the water of the Word! Keep pressing in. As you go about your day, God will remind you of the things you have absorbed in the Word. Jesus said, "The Holy Spirit, whom the Father will send in My name, will teach you all things and will remind you of everything I have said to you" (John 14:26 NIV). This allows us to make all of our decisions based on the Word of God. Whether we are deciding whom to marry, where to move, or which job to take, we are able to look at the Word for reference and *rest assured* that God has given us a green light.

The Word of God has never been more available than it is today in our western world. Whether you prefer leather-bound paper or a digital app like *YouVersion*, I encourage you to start somewhere. I usually recommend starting with the book of Mark in the New Testament. It's a short gospel that provides a beautiful look into the life and work of Jesus. Set a measurable, realistic reading plan and partner with the Holy Spirit as you go about it.

Confess the Scriptures daily, letting them saturate your mindset, perceptions, beliefs, thoughts, words and actions. Make His Word your mediation. I cannot emphasize enough the value of making the Word of God your own. See the promises in the Bible as inheritances assigned to you by God. In so doing, you will begin to read them in the first person. For example, Paul said, "And my God will meet all your needs according to the riches of His glory in Christ Jesus" (Philippians 4:19). When the Bible is personal, you can convert it to the *first person* and say, "God will meet all of *(fill in your name)'s* needs, according to the riches..."

When someone addresses you in a text message, a letter or an email, you know that what they are saying was targeted to you *specifically* and *personally*. Likewise, understand that the Word of God is His letter written to you *specifically* and *personally*. To separate the voice of God from the Bible itself is to fail to maximize the potential of this great Book. The Word of God is our standard plumb line, and, in many ways, the most consistent way in which God speaks to His people.

THE **NON-NEGOTIABLES**

- *The Word of God* plainly displays the exact *will of God* pertaining to life and godliness.
- God is *actively speaking* through His Word by highlighting insights to guide you in your present circumstances.
- The Word of God is a seed that is implanted in our hearts and minds, growing to produce fruit. (See Mark 4:26-29.)
- Interacting with the Holy Spirit is a *necessary* activity in your daily Bible reading.

REFLECTION QUESTIONS

Pray, Ask and Listen: Flip through your Bible or the Bible app on your phone and ask God to highlight a specific passage to you. This may come as a flowing thought, mental picture, inner knowing or a sense you get about a specific chapter and verse that seems to stand out to you as you flip through your Bible or scroll through your Bible app. After that, ask God to speak to you through it. Write down what you sense He is saying to you through the Scripture. (See page 20, 4th paragraph.)

_____
_____
_____
_____
_____

This chapter states, "...daily choices and acts of faith will trigger, activate and cause God's favor, blessings and breakthrough in your life...as you [become] *a doer of the Word*." (See page 25.) Pray, Ask and Listen: Are there Scriptures that you've merely heard but not *done*? What are the negative effects of hearing God through His Word but failing to act on it?

_____
_____
_____
_____
_____
_____

You would not play organized sports without training, practice and setting a plan. (See page 19.) Likewise, we shouldn't attempt to walk by faith without a fundamental plan. Below, write a plan for partaking of the Word of God daily—intentionally leaning into His voice from the Scriptures. Outline your goals, passages you would like to study, and a reasonable schedule for engaging with the Bible.

_____
_____
_____
_____
_____
_____

Pleasing God is an impossibility without *faith*. (See page 27.) Hearing, receiving and obeying His voice can *only* be done on the avenue of faith. What does this look like? What corresponding actions do you need to take to obey what God has spoken to *you personally* in His Word? Document below:

_____
_____
_____
_____
_____
_____

ACTIVATION DECREE

I decree and declare that I am enriched with an appetite for the Word of God. I speak hunger into my soul and grace to set a plan to partake of the living Scriptures daily. I receive God's wisdom, revelation, insight, and understanding and I will draw it from the well of the Word of God by faith. I will enter a lifestyle of being nourished by the manna of the Word. May the Holy Spirit Himself remind me of that which is written, when I need it the most! In Jesus Name Amen!

SETTING **EXPECTATIONS**

In the days, weeks and months to come, you should:

- Use some *or all* of the 7 practical tips laid out in the chapter and develop a holy habit of daily Bible reading.
- Intentionally search out Scriptures that God highlights and speaks to you.

- Cultivate your heart and mind to be *good soil* for the seed of the Word to be planted.
- Write down impressions, passages and interactions you have with the Holy Spirit while studying your Bible.

Feel free to write out further goals, expectations and God encounters in the space below:

3

PRAYER (PART 1)
CHAPTER THREE ACTIVATION GUIDE

A TWO-WAY DIALOG WITH GOD

Prayer is not complicated. There are no special levers to pull or passwords to use. Simply put, prayer happens *anytime* you turn your heart to communicate with God. We are to pray boldly, transparently and with desperation for God in our hearts. He lives in us! Yet, far too often, we pray to a God we feel is distant. We pray, say *amen*, and then dart off to go about our daily routines. However, the fullness of prayer can only be experienced when we pause to hear back from heaven. Prayer is a *dialog* not a monologue. It's a two-way street of communication between you and God. I truly believe that God wants to speak to you more than you want to hear from Him!

Prayer is the hotspot for hearing God. For example, the best way to hear from a person is to engage them in conversation. In that same way, the best way to hear from God is to engage Him! James said, "Come near to God and He will come near to you" (James 4:8). As you do, you will unlock visual, auditory and kinetic experiences in prayer. Before you pull out a dictionary, I'd like to briefly explain each one and what they entail.

1. VISUAL: An inner visual experience in prayer can range from seeing an image, a video, a vision, text or words spontaneously within your mind. They aren't conjured up or merely imagined but placed in your inner mind by God. It could be given for a prayer assignment, a direction for the future, or guidance for a decision at hand. Often, you might see these visual images superimposed in the natural world, in which your eyes are open, where you actually see something interlaced with the real world—sort of like a hologram. Concerning God's voice, Jesus expressed our need to have *eyes to see*, referring to this visual realm.

2. INNER AUDITORY: This method often shows up in the form of flowing thoughts in your mind that are accompanied by a sense of peace, hope and wisdom. If a thought is accompanied by fear, dread or confusion, it is not the voice of God! Often, when God speaks in an inner auditory manner, you will sense the still, small voice of God whispering within you. This reflects the Bible's emphasis on having *ears to hear*. Hearing an inner auditory whisper from God in prayer can be subtle. As a result, many brush it off as their own stream of consciousness. However, as we lean in and grow in these methods, we will find God dropping loving phrases and relevant truths consistently.

3. KINETIC: The word *kinetic* in science involves *motion*. Hearing from God in a *kinetic* way involves God's voice *moving* in you in a way that causes physical manifestations. For example, if God speaks to you in a kinetic way, you might experience a sense of peace, joy, comfort, goosebumps, tingling, warm sensations, watering eyes or other types of physical senses that come through spiritual experiences and encounters with God's presence. These senses can also come with an inward knowing or an impression you get about what you are feeling and sensing.

These three realities are closer to being real in your life than you might think. Take some time to read the Word of God out loud—namely the passages concerning His voice. Pray in faith, not in doubt. Confess with thanksgiving that you *will* experience His voice on many levels. Thanksgiving is absolutely foundational to experiencing the voice of God in prayer. Paul actually told us that thanksgiving is an ingredient to mix into *all* types of prayer. (See Philippians 4:6.) Too often, we wait to thank God until *after* we see something manifest. Yet this demonstrates a lack of faith. For instance, if I tell my six-year-old godson on Monday that I am taking him to a waterpark on Friday, he is going to praise and thank me all week for taking him to the waterpark. He is also going to tell anyone who will listen, with excitement, that his Uncle Sterling is taking him to the waterpark on Friday. What is he doing? He is *believing*, or having *faith* in my word to him, and he has received in his little heart that he will be going to the waterpark on Friday.

Likewise, God wants us to have childlike faith and thanksgiving *ahead of time*. Thank Him for His voice and activity even before you sense or feel it. Thank Him with expectation, listen for His speaking. Relax and don't overthink it. It's a continual process that you are able to fine tune. For example, I can be in a crowd of one hundred people but if my mom says my name, I recognize it over the crowd's noise. Why? Because of the intimate knowledge I have built with her over the years. It's the same thing when it comes to hearing God's voice. As you develop in the Spirit, He will train your senses to hear Him over the noises and distractions.

What are those noises and distractions? At times they may be other people, ourselves, the flesh and often—the enemy. It's important to know what the enemy's voice sounds like. To *extinguish* the enemy's voice, we must *distinguish* the enemy's voice. When we refer to the enemy, we are referring to the demonic spiritual realm of the devil, evil spirits and demons. It is essential to understand that the devil himself, also known as satan, is NOT equal to God whatsoever. He is a created being. His authority has been stripped and his only weapon is to throw out "what if's" and "yeah but's" toward the promises of God. In prayer, I used to wonder, *Am I good enough? Do I have what it takes to fulfill my calling?* Doubt, anxiety, fear and confusion would enter my mind. I'm sure many of you can relate. While prayer is a hotspot for God's activity, it can also attract unseen forces that attempt to disrupt what God is doing. Shake off these threats and holdfast to the presence and promise of Jesus.

Throughout your day, *practice the presence of God.* Use simple acknowledgements such as, "I worship You, Lord. I honor You. Thank You, Jesus. Bless You, God." These simple recognitions of God at work will keep you aware of His presence and will thwart the attempts of the enemy. Ask questions like, "Lord, what are You saying about this situation? Lord, what do You want me to do in response to these circumstances? Jesus, what is the truth about this challenge I am facing?" Then listen and allow Him to speak to your mind and heart.

Be patient in hearing from Him. Waiting on the Lord in prayer is a biblical practice that we can so easily neglect in our fast-paced world if we are not intentional about connecting to God's voice. God's broadcasting system is always on and operational. God's voice is generally at the same volume and frequency. It's just that things rise above His sound and disturb the frequency, impairing your clarity in hearing Him. Lean in and trust Him to speak. He is more eager than you think.

THE **NON-NEGOTIABLES**

- Prayer is a *dialog* not a *monologue*.
- The presence of God is to be continually *practiced*. Divine exchange is not a one-time experience but a cultivated lifestyle.
- To *extinguish* the enemy's voice, we must *distinguish* the enemy's voice.
- Hearing from God in prayer is something we can increase. Embrace the process and your growth will be exponential.

REFLECTION QUESTIONS

In prayer, God can speak to us in a *visual* way. He also speaks in an *inner auditory* or *kinetic* manner. (See page 49-50.) In the coming days and weeks, be mindful of these three inlets for the voice of God and journal your experiences with each, based on the chapter's description of their function.

_____
_____
_____
_____
_____
_____

The chapter encourages you to ask three questions to the Lord and then listen for an answer. (See page 73.) Ask the questions individually, wait for a reply, and journal the response in the lines provided. "Jesus, how do You see me? Jesus, what gifts do You see in me? Jesus, what do You love about me?"

_____
_____
_____
_____
_____
_____

Thanksgiving positions us to receive God's voice, yet we are to be thankful for what God gives, by faith, before we see the manifestation. (See page 49.) Set high expectations for hearing God, and thank Him for fulfilling them. Pray, Ask and Listen: Write out your *thanksgiving* list and develop gratitude so that God will bring it to pass.

_____
_____
_____
_____
_____
_____

ACTIVATION DECREE

I decree and declare that my prayer life will not be a one-way venting session but a rich, fulfilling, powerful two-way line of communication between me and God. By faith, may the Spirit of God activate Me visually, auditorily and kinetically to experience His voice in prayer, from this day forward! In Jesus Name Amen!

SETTING **EXPECTATIONS**

In the days, weeks, and months to come, you should:

- Use your ears in prayer as much as you use your mouth.
- Practice God's presence by relaxing and opening yourself to what He might say.
- Patiently wait on the Lord. Don't be rushed in the secret place.
- Cultivate a lifestyle of gratitude. Thanksgiving will position you for increase in your *experiential* faith walk.

Feel free to write out further goals, expectations and God experiences in the space below:

_____
_____
_____
_____
_____
_____
_____
_____
_____
_____
_____
_____
_____

4

PRAYER (PART 2)
CHAPTER THREE ACTIVATION GUIDE

A CONTINUED CONVERSATION

Throughout Scriptures, we see people *inquiring of the Lord*. David said, "One thing have I asked of the LORD, that will I seek after: that I may dwell in the house of the LORD all the days of my life, to gaze upon the beauty of the LORD and to inquire in His temple" (Psalm 27:4). David had a simple mission: to be in God's presence, to stare at His beauty and to inquire of Him. We often discuss the value of dwelling in God's presence. We have countless worship songs about the beauty of the Lord. Yet *inquiring* of the Lord in prayer is a lesser discussed topic. However, it's a vitally important one.

Asking questions does two things: first, it produces humility within us. When we ask questions, we are simultaneously admitting that we don't have the full answer and that we want and value God's perspective. Second, it sets us up to hear a response! When a person complains about never hearing the Lord's voice, I would ask, "When did you last ask Him a question?" On page 82 in *How to Hear God*, I provide a long list of creative inquiries to make of the Lord. Here are just a handful:

- What's on Your heart, God?
- Where should I go today? Will You help me plan out my day?
- Are there steps of faith I need to take to receive breakthrough and manifestation in this area of my life?
- Jesus, if my heart were a house, is there any room You would like to redecorate? Why?

Upon asking these things, ready yourself to hear from Him. Inquiring of the Lord should work its way beyond just you and Jesus. In fact, on a daily basis, I ask God to guide me in every conversation that I have with other people. I usually say short prayers in my mind or under my breath, such as, "Holy Spirit, guide me in this conversation." Often, I find that God will speak to me about a person or reveal something in their heart. This will allow me to pray for them and steer the conversation accordingly. Many times, I've heard from the Lord about something only He could know, brought it up to the person I was meeting with, and was able to minister to them accordingly. Simple prayers under your breath, combined with listening closely, allows you to minister to others in practical, powerful and effective ways.

Inquiring of the Lord is a daily lifestyle. In addition to spending quality alone time with God, the two-way conversations I have with Him throughout my day-to-day life have built the greatest sense of companionship and intimacy with Him. One of the most common statements I hear people make is that they feel as though they don't have time to pray and that their lives are so hectic and busy, it is hard to spend quality alone time with God—often coupling them together as one. This is a common misunderstanding of prayer. Prayer, as we stated earlier, is any communication with God. Question: Do you have the time to talk to yourself during the day? Yes, of course you do! We all have a continual inner dialogue going on in our minds every day, all day. The area in which I've underestimated God most is in connecting Him to the internal communication of my everyday life. God is in the everyday with you! You need only turn this inner dialogue toward a conversation with God. This is vital to living a life filled with joy, peace and God's voice.

Now inner conversations with God are the bulk of my communication with Him and they occur throughout my day. On the days I don't get to spend quality alone time with Him, for whatever reason, I can always continually connect with Him throughout my day. Putting this revelation into practice in your daily life will greatly increase how much you hear God's voice. I hear God's voice every single day of my life, and you can too!

Making *quality quiet time alone with God* a vital part of your spiritual life is foundational in hearing God's voice. You could call it the secret place, the throne room or just sitting with the Lord. When I first began to do this, I found that my mind would drift, as it still does at times. When your mind drifts, give yourself plenty of grace. Beating yourself up won't help the situation. Steady yourself back on Jesus and let your mind and affection float to Him.

We truly can't underestimate the value of spending time with the Lord in solitude. Attempting to hear from God without ever spending time with Him is like *using* the Lord for His voice and guidance. Yet, the Lord is not meant to be used but loved. Jesus, Himself, understood this, as Mark 14 describes Him dismissing the crowd to spend time alone, praying and seeking His Father.

This alone time with God can take many forms. I've sat in silence and I've also sat with worship music to aid in the process. Don't go in with preconceived notions. There are times when God and I laugh, have fun and it is so light-hearted that I feel like I am hanging out with my best friend. At other times, I find myself crying and weeping, overcome by His love and His Presence. Every encounter is different. The most important thing is that you make time for Him.

To be honest with you, busyness is one of the greatest silent killers of intimacy with God, yourself, your family and those closest to you. It is just as big as any addiction, idol, habit or self-destructive cycle that we can have, and for most of us, busyness is socially acceptable and sometimes even celebrated. Learn to clear the schedule, make time for Jesus and reap the benefits. One of the rewards that was so profound for me was when I realized that the more time I spent alone with God in times of solitude, *the less lonely I felt.*

Many ask how fasting plays into this spiritual life. It plays a mighty role. Fasting has its own frequency, if you will. It provides us with benefits that, frankly, nothing else can. Fasting has been a huge part of my walk with God. It has been vital to building up my spirit-man and tearing down the self-willed flesh, thus, allowing my mind, will and emotions to be governed and under control of the Holy Spirit. Now, fasting is not about currying favor with God or earning tools from Him. Instead, it's about silencing the flesh and aligning yourself with sole dependency on Him.

Contrary to popular opinion, fasting is not about giving up food. In fact, it's not about food at all. It's about Jesus. It's not about what you give up and it is not a spiritual diet. It's about aligning yourself with the Lord and redirecting your hunger to the living God. It's about subduing the flesh and positioning yourself to hear from God and entering into new spiritual realms.

Fasting looks different for everyone. You could give up or cut back from playing mindless games on your phone, TV, internet, soda, coffee, sugar, bread, video games, social media, limit meals to once a day, eat vegetables only and so on. Step out as you are led and set aside what needs to be set aside—it will most assuredly produce supernatural results in your life. I did a forty-day fast which you can read about starting on page 101 in *How to Hear God*. I was hesitant at first but then had clear confirmation that it was from the Lord. God supernaturally strengthened me during the fast. I'm not just referring to spiritual insight and inner strength but actual physical strength. In fact, on the last day, I took measurements and I was in shock. I had lost body fat but, supernaturally, I had *gained* lean muscle mass! I was so thankful and blown away.

Another benefit of fasting paired with prayer is the ability to practice taking thoughts captive. We are commanded to do so in Scripture but what does this really look like? For me, I use what I call the RCRP method, which stands for *Refuse, Confess, Repent, Pray*. When a negative thought enters my mind, I refuse it and push back. I slap down the thought. From there, I confess out loud, standing my ground. I say, "I am a child of God. I declare that this thought has no room in the holy ground of my mind." Third, I repent, which means to change the way I think. I literally turn from one direction to another, mentally. Finally, *I pray*. I connect with God in my words and allow His thoughts to become *one* with mine. I seek Him and open my heart to hear His voice. Sometimes, the negative thought is toward a person in the form of unforgiveness. Other times it's fear over a situation or perhaps even self-doubt. Regardless, learn to bless the person, bless the situation, bless yourself, and bless God in prayer. Avail yourself to all forms of consistent prayer and you will find that hearing God comes with ease.

THE **NON-NEGOTIABLES**

- *Inquiring* of the Lord often precedes *receiving* from the Lord.
- Learn to hear God in your *daily interactions* with others.
- Our daily internal dialogue can be turned into a continual conversation and constant connection with God.
- Busyness is one of the greatest *silent killers* of intimacy with God.
- Fasting is not about earning God's affection but, instead, *aligning* yourself with His voice.
- *Refuse, Confess, Repent, Pray* is a winning formula to conquer all negative thinking.

REFLECTION QUESTIONS

Inquiry toward God is not to be forgotten. (See page 81.) Are there things you have never asked God but would like to? Write down those questions and make it a point to pray, listen and lean into His wisdom on the matter, both in the Scriptures and in His active voice. Record your findings moving forward.

_____
_____
_____
_____
_____
_____

As I developed a heart to hear God for others, there began to be a wise and loving flow to my conversations, interactions on my job, emails, texts, posts on social media, and advice that I would give to family, friends and others. (See page 86.) Write out the names of those you interact with on a weekly basis and make it a point to share God's heart with them. Pray, Ask and Listen: Write out what you feel God might be saying to them or how God might be leading you to encourage them.

_____
_____
_____
_____
_____
_____

Everyone has an internal dialogue. (See page 46.) We ask questions, think through issues, debate with ourselves and compare pros and cons internally. Inviting God into this continual, daily inner dialogue opens us to hearing Him at a new level and frequency. In the coming days, when you catch yourself in an internal dialogue, actively invite God into it. Record the experience of how God shifted your internal conversation:

_____
_____
_____
_____
_____
_____

I wrote in the chapter that busyness is a killer of intimacy with Jesus. We can even be busy with good things, not necessarily sin and compromise. Are there things in your life that could be removed from the schedule in order to clear up time for intimacy with Jesus? Pray, Ask and Listen: Write them below and outline actionable steps to take to make this happen:

_____
_____
_____
_____
_____
_____

ACTIVATION DECREE

I decree and declare that the inquiries from my heart and responses from God's heart will begin to become normal in my life. I will leverage the power of prayer to change my world and become a regular recipient of the voice of the Lord. In Jesus Name Amen!

SETTING EXPECTATIONS

In the days, weeks, and months to come, you should:

- Make daily creative inquiries of the Lord, taking time to *listen* to His response.
- Intentionally *lean into* God's voice when communicating with others.
- As you are led, fast and pray for a given amount of time. Journal your experiences.

- Refine the art of taking thoughts captive and consecrating your mind to Jesus.

Feel free to write out further goals, expectations and God experiences in the space below:

_____
_____
_____
_____
_____
_____
_____
_____
_____
_____
_____
_____
_____

5

THE HOLY SPIRIT
CHAPTER FOUR ACTIVATION GUIDE

THE ACTIVE AGENT ON EARTH

The Holy Spirit *is* God. He is not an "it" or some mysterious wind. He is the Third Person of the Trinity, which consists of God the Father; God the Son, Jesus Christ; and the Holy Spirit. Our singular God is *Three in One*. It would be a serious injustice to unpack the topic of hearing God's voice without introducing you to the vital role of the Holy Spirit in that process. As believers, the Holy Spirit dwells in us. We are God's address and residence—the temple for His presence! (See 1 Corinthians 6:19-20.) God sees lost souls as prime real estate. When we call upon Jesus, we hand Him the keys and He moves in by the Spirit!

This means that the same Holy Spirit whom Jesus had is now living inside of you. The question is: *What is He doing in there?* He certainly is not with us just to take up space. For starters, He is making us like Jesus. From the inside out, the Holy Spirit transforms us, refines us and sharpens our character in every way. He inspires us to worship and provides us with encouragement. He comforts us and mends us. The Greek language describes Him as our ever present *parakletos*, which means *One who comes alongside us*. Many times, when I'm in prayer over a situation, I will hear a voice within me say things like, "I've got you. I'm with you. Trust Me." This is the Holy Spirit giving me encouragement and comfort—perhaps you can relate.

Many people say, "Oh, I wish I could walk with Jesus physically like the disciples did." While this would be an incredible experience, the presence of the Holy Spirit is actually an upgrade to what the disciples had. Jesus said, "It's better that I go, so the Holy Spirit can come" (John 16:7). How can this be true? Because Jesus limited Himself to a physical body, yet the Spirit is with us, 24/7/365, always willing and ready to speak and guide.

Because of His *ever-present* nature, we are to be in constant communion and fellowship with the Holy Spirit. If God were still on the earth in a physical way, we would have to physically walk to where He was to bow down and worship Him. Yet God is here by His Spirit, and we can access His heart and voice *anywhere, anytime.* Learn to take full advantage of His residing presence. When I am making a decision on something, I will defer to the Holy Spirit to see if I have a green light or not.

If I have what I call a *check in my spirit,* I will put the decision on hold. Usually, it comes in the form of an uneasiness in my stomach or chest. Some call it a *gut feeling, mother's intuition* or a *sixth sense*. However it occurs, we know it to be the leading of the voice of the Holy Spirit. When you know something is right, you will have a sense of unmistakable peace and tranquility from the Holy Spirit within you. Paul said, "Let the peace of Christ rule (act as umpire continually) in your hearts" (Galatians 3:15 AMPC). This means that *peace* calls the shots!

This is one of the primary manifestations of the voice of the Holy Spirit.

When we neglect the inner voice of the Holy Spirit, we are, by default, going to seek after another voice. Often, we take counsel from our own souls (our mind, will and emotions). This is our attempt at running on self-will and human intuition, which leads us nowhere near God's best for our lives. We may also take counsel from the demonic realm—meaning we buy into lies, deception and temptations with decision making. Not only that, but when we neglect the Spirit's leading, we risk unknowingly taking guidance from the world, meaning we take our cues from the media, movies, culture, worldly advice and earthly wisdom. We can save so much headache and heartache by clinging to the peaceful inner voice of the Holy Spirit.

THE BAPTISM IN THE HOLY SPIRIT

The phrase *baptism in the Holy Spirit* has been widely used and taught for ages in the church. There is plenty of misinformation floating in Christian culture about it, so I'd like to briefly provide you with a clear overview. For a more detailed understanding, I recommend reading my full explanation on the subject starting on page 145 in *How to Hear God*. The baptism in the Holy Spirit is a God-given experience that takes place either at the time of salvation *or*, often, after salvation. In this experience, the Holy Spirit completely submerses you with Himself and empowers you in a dynamic, fresh and unique way.

You might think, *I thought all believers had the Holy Spirit.* Yes, all believers have the Holy Spirit, yet not all have been *baptized* in the Holy Spirit. In Acts 2, 120 believers who had the Holy Spirit living in them were gathered and *filled*, or *baptized*, in the Holy Spirit. In Acts 19, Paul asked a few Christians if they had received the baptism in the Spirit since they first believed—they had not. He fixed that, real quickly, and God filled them with the Holy Spirit. The difference between receiving the Holy Spirit at salvation and receiving the subsequent *baptism* in the Holy Spirit is sort of like the difference between having water splashed on you and being thrown into the ocean. The baptism in the Spirit is a *complete submersion.*

After Jesus baptized me with the Holy Spirit, my relationship with God greatly *increased*. The Scriptures came alive in a new way, I was emboldened, revelation began flowing and I was empowered supernaturally. Not only that but I also received my heavenly prayer language and began *speaking in tongues*. Now, I grew up in a conservative Christian denomination that taught against this, to which many can relate. As a result, there is a certain stigma that surrounds praying in tongues. Let me assure you that it is a wonderful gift from God, with loads of scriptural backing. The apostle Paul writes, "The one who prays using a private 'prayer language' certainly gets a lot out of it" (1 Corinthians 14:4 MSG). I want to encourage you to yield yourself over to whatever Jesus wants to do in and through your life, including praying in tongues!

How do you receive this baptism in the Spirit and speak with other tongues? The *same way* you received salvation...by faith! Here's a quick breakdown of the process.

1. RECOGNIZE

First, you have to see from Scripture that it is the will of God for you to be filled with the Spirit. Faith comes by hearing the Word (see Romans 10), so search out those passages and get them inside of you! Jesus said, "If mere men know how to give good gifts to their children, how much more will the Father give the Holy Spirit to those who ask?" (Matthew 7:11 PARA).

2. RELAX

Get into a place that is distraction-free. Let self-consciousness melt off of you. So often, we overthink the process and block our spirits from receiving from God. As we begin praying in tongues, we wonder, *Is this me? Is this God? Is this all in my head?* Let yourself relax and become available to whatever God might want to do.

3. REQUEST

Ask God, in faith, *"Lord, I thank You that Your Word says if I ask that I will receive, that if I seek then I will find and if I knock the door will be open to me. I am asking, right now, in faith, for You, Jesus, to baptize me in the Holy Spirit and for the gift of praying in tongues, Holy Spirit I ask You to infill me with Your power! I receive this right now, by faith in Your Word. In Jesus' name. Amen."*

4. RECEIVE

After asking God for this precious gift, take the actionable step of opening your mouth, yielding it over the Holy Spirit and speak words that are not known to you. Many think that praying in tongues will overtake you. Paul actually said, "If I pray in an unknown tongue, my spirit prays" (1 Corinthians 14:14). Notice he said, "If *I* pray." He did the praying. Likewise, in Acts too: "*They began* to speak with tongues" (Acts 2:4). They got the ball rolling. When you let these sounds and syllables rise up from your heart, you will begin saying phrases in another language. It's much like a garden hose; you decide when to turn it on, but when you do—it simply *flows*.

Once you begin praying in tongues, continue to do so! As with any language, practice is important. Don't believe the lies of the enemy, telling you that it's trivial or in your head. Command all other voices to cease. Studies have been done on this extensively and they found that when a person prays in tongues, the part of their brain responsible for language is completely inactive. In other words, it's a divine flow from your spirit! Pray in tongues between twenty minutes and an hour per day—more if you can.

You might wonder, *What does this have to do with hearing the voice of God?* When we pray in tongues, the Holy Spirit is providing us with the utterance. God, Himself, is supplying the sounds and syllables. Paul said when you pray in tongues, "Pray that you may interpret" (1 Corinthians 14:13). This means God will help you decipher the language you're using at times with impressions, thoughts, ideas, images or insights that come to your natural mind while praying in tongues. The interpretation is not as important as the practice and lifestyle of praying in tongues. Sometimes, I don't get an interpretation, but I don't let that hinder me from praying in tongues. We have to trust the Holy Spirit to pray effectively through us.

Again, make it a point to pray in the Spirit daily. Fellowship with the Holy Spirit and develop a habit of journaling with the Holy Spirit. Spend time with Him and write out the flow of what's on His heart. Don't be afraid to get it wrong. As you make a habit of this, you will look back at the rich tapestry of the Holy Spirit's voice and involvement in your life.

A COMMON HINDRANCE

There are very few things that can hinder your ability to experience the Holy Spirit quite like *unforgiveness*. In a book on hearing God, you might wonder how forgiveness fits in. See, when we hold grudges, we actually hold ourselves captive. We actively step out of God's frequency when we live in bitterness. The Holy Spirit is the one who nudges us to a place of forgiveness and purity of heart. As He does, it opens our spiritual receptors to experiencing God's voice with more clarity than ever.

A simple prayer goes a long way: *"Holy Spirit, bring to my heart and mind who or what I need to forgive and release over to You."* Then listen for the Holy Spirit to speak to you and bring things to your heart and mind. Once you see the person or people you are to forgive, confess that you forgive them, *out loud*. Say, "Lord, I forgive _____ in Jesus' name, and I release that person and situation over to You. Thank You for cleansing my heart."

You might not *feel* it entirely, but it's a faith thing! From there, ask God to fill you up in those areas that were once occupied by bitterness. Releasing a grudge can leave a void that the Holy Spirit Himself will fill. Finally, *bless that person*. This may be the most difficult step but it can be the most freeing step! Pray that God would bless them abundantly in every way. Choose to declare God's goodness over them. Jesus said, "When you are mistreated and harassed by others, accept it as your mission to pray for them" (Luke 6:28 TPT).

I call this the *unforgiveness purge*, and it's one of the most important activities we can practice as believers. It's a continual process for us as we journey through life and navigate offense, hurt and trauma. Let the Holy Spirit bring things to your awareness and deal with them accordingly. In so doing, you will position yourself to hear God with more clarity and frequency than ever!

THE **NON-NEGOTIABLES**

- The Holy Spirit is the *active agent* on the earth who inhabits, empowers and energizes the believer and the Word of God.
- The Holy Spirit often leads through a *sense of peace* over a decision.
- The baptism in the Holy Spirit, coupled with the feature and benefit of praying in tongues, is an *enhancement* to your Christian life that God desires for everyone.
- *Unforgiveness* will hinder your ability to experience all that God has for you. Purge it from your heart as often as needed.

REFLECTION QUESTIONS

You likely have a major decision(s) on the horizon. We all have them at some point. The Holy Spirit wants to guide you through a sense of peace to make the right decision. (See page 143.) Actively ask the Holy Spirit to give you a peace, or a sense of unsettledness, about the decisions at hand. Write down your findings and the results of your decisions.

_____
_____
_____
_____
_____

The baptism in the Holy Spirit is mentioned in all four Gospels in the Bible. (See page 146.) In the book of Acts, new believers are filled with the Spirit and seasoned believers are re-filled with the Spirit. Take time to recognize, relax, request and receive the Holy Spirit, either anew or afresh. Write down your experience and how it will impact you moving forward.

_____

_____

_____

_____

_____

_____

Unforgiveness is a soul-disease that has afflicted many. (See page 168.) Pray, Ask and Listen: Do you have offense in your heart? Are there people who you need to release? As you pray through these things with the Holy Spirit's help, write out the person(s) name and make a written plan to pray for them and bless them. Furthermore, write out the many benefits one may experience from walking in forgiveness.

_____

_____

_____

_____

_____

_____

ACTIVATION DECREE

I decree and declare that the Holy Spirit will be more real in my life than ever. May the grace of God empower me to give attention, time and affection to the ever-present Holy Spirit. My senses are being heightened and my spirit, soul and body will be more aware than ever of the Spirit within me! In Jesus Name Amen!

SETTING EXPECTATIONS

In the days, weeks and months to come, you should:

- Increase your awareness of the Third Person of the Trinity.
- If you haven't already, pray for God to baptize you in the Holy Spirit. If you have in the past, receive a fresh baptism in the Spirit by faith.
- Using notes on your phone or a physical journal, begin to document your journey with the Holy Spirit.
- Whether you're a newbie or a veteran in the faith, practice a forgiveness purge and guard your heart from offense.

Feel free to write out further goals, expectations and God encounters in the space below:

_____
_____
_____
_____
_____

STERLING HARRIS

> 6
>
> # THE INWARD WITNESS
> CHAPTER FIVE ACTIVATION GUIDE

GOD'S SPIRIT IN YOUR SPIRIT

God is *Three-in-One*—Father, Son, Holy Spirit. From the get-go, the Scriptures tell us that we are made in His image. As a result, we *also* are *three-in-one*. You *are* a spirit who *lives* in a body and *has* a soul. As a triune person, it's important to know the function of your whole being—spirit, soul, and body.

Your spirit (often called the *heart* in the Bible) is the *real you*. This is your eternal being, which has been born again and will eventually leave your body when you graduate from this life to the next. Your spirit is redeemed and perfect before God. In fact, it's the dwelling place of God and is connected to the Holy Spirit.

You spirit connected with and led by the Holy Spirit within you is the "inward witness" that we refer to. Your body *contains* your spirit. The body is your temporal "earth suit," which allows you to function physically on the earth. Your *soul* is composed of your mental faculties. The soul is the mind, will and human emotions. The soul is neither good nor bad—it looks like whatever we feed it. As Christians, we are to *renew* our minds (see Romans 12:2) so that our soul looks more like our spirit and less like our flesh.

Having given you a brief map of your being, I'd like to hone in on the function of your spirit—*your inward witness*. Your spirit acts as an internal compass. A GPS is a navigation system that stands for *Global Positioning System*. In other words, it tells you where you are upon the globe. Your spirit is a navigation system that tells you where you are in the will of God. You have Holy Ghost Google Maps inside of you, directing and leading you. Your spirit will lead you by an abundance of peace or by a lack of peace, in accordance with your thoughts, words and decisions.

You might wonder, *What does this feel like?* The best way to describe it is a *gut feeling*. See, your spirit is located in your midsection. It's not in your foot. It's not in your hand. In fact, Jesus said, "He that believeth on me...out of his *belly* shall flow rivers of living water" (John 7:38 KJV). *The New American Standard Bible* says, "Out of his *innermost being*,"—this is the human spirit. You've likely heard people say, "Follow your gut," or "I have a good gut feeling about it." They are responding to the activity taking place in their spirit.

For example, when you do things that you know are not right, you will often get a sense of uneasiness, a lack of peace in your stomach or a tightness in your chest area. That is your spirit alerting you to something that needs to be addressed or brought to the Lord in prayer so that certain actions can be taken or avoided. When we push past an unsettledness in our spirits and make a decision that our hearts don't agree with, we pay a price. It's like driving through a red light because you emotionally want it to be green. The inward witness is a reliable measuring stick for major life decisions as well as small day-to-day adventures.

The best way we can assure that we are being *led* correctly is by being sure we are *fed* correctly. If we fill up on garbage, doubt, unbelief, and worldly things, we will develop a divided heart. As a result, trusting our inward witness will be difficult because of static, emotion and distraction that keeps us from hearing correctly. We must align ourselves with God and His Word, keeping our spirits pure before Him. My personal declaration has been: "I make it my aim and goal in life to get my heart to a place where it has no will of its own, except for the will of God."

As we do this, we will experience a sold-out devotion, a singular focus, a heart that's clear and guidance from the inside that comes easily in *any* situation. We were designed by God to live this way from the inside out. See, there are two different types of knowledge. There is *factual head knowledge,* in which people say, "I know God exists and I believe in Him." Then there is *heart knowledge,* which says, "I know God and talk with Him about my life every day because I have *experienced* His power, love and favor in a personal, real, and intimate way!" Both are important, however, it is the *experiential* knowledge of God's love every day that separates religious duty from relationship. The best way to steward our hearts is to allow the knowledge in our head to make that 21-inch jump to our hearts.

As you do this and live out your daily life, leaning on the inward witness of the Holy Spirit, God will guide you. The inward witness will give you:

- Impressions in your heart
- Subtle nudges
- A sense of inward peace or uneasiness

- A quickening
- Spiritual/mental downloads
- Prevailing thoughts
- Flowing thoughts
- Flashbacks

One of the best ways to clarify an important decision is to *check your spirit.* Checking your spirit is a means to ensure that the decisions you're making are bearing witness to the inner peace of God's Spirit within you. Discernment can often be a part of the inward check. To put it simply, discernment is a *positive* or *negative* perception, feeling or sense you get about someone or some situation.

Let me provide a caveat. Discernment is *not* suspicion. It is not a worldly, fleshly, self-willed judgment. It's not based on outward appearances and preconceived notions. You will find that a situation may look great on the outside but you discern something uneasy taking place, and, as it turns out, the whole thing was wrong. On the other hand, a situation might look grim on the outside but you discern that God is at work, and it turns out to be incredible. The only way to be sure our discernment about a person, situation or circumstance is *sound* is to filter our inward witness through the lens of God's love.

As we walk in love and regularly feed our hearts with good things, God will lead our hearts by His Spirit. Paul said, "For in Him we live, and move, and have our being" (Acts 17:28 KJV). In this reality, you will be constantly leaning on, following and being sensitive to the inward witness of the Holy Spirit living on the inside of you!

THE **NON-NEGOTIABLES**

- You are a three-part being: spirit, soul and body—each of which can play a role in hearing God.
- Your spirit is your innermost being and is inhabited by the Holy Spirit which is the inward witness, that guides, leads and calls important shots.
- To steward our hearts well, we must feed our hearts well. In this, we will be positioned to hear God without confusion and division.
- *Discernment* is a God-given ability to judge a situation properly *in love*. Don't confuse it with *suspicion* or carnal judgement.

REFLECTION QUESTIONS

Having a gut feeling about something is unmistakable. We know biblically that this is our inward witness. (See page 173.) Have you experienced this? Recall a time when you either disobeyed this *inward witness* or obeyed it. What was the outcome and how can you learn from it moving forward?

As discussed, the inward witness can result in impressions, prevailing thoughts, spiritual downloads and so forth. (See page 178.) Over the next few days, take note of the activity in your spirit and watch to see if it resembles these manifestations. Document your experience and the outcomes.

_____
_____
_____
_____
_____
_____

Every believer has been given a measure of *discernment*. (See page 180.) To not use discernment is to be oblivious and vulnerable. Pray, Ask and Listen: Are there situations in your life that you have not discerned properly? Are there relationships, ventures, thought patterns or opportunities for which you need better discernment? *Check your spirit*, write out your findings, then take the necessary actions.

_____
_____
_____
_____
_____
_____

ACTIVATION DECREE

I decree and declare that a new measure of sensitivity to the inward witness will be found in me. I will be fed and led with excellence all the days of my life. May the singular focus of my spirit be on Jesus and provide me with the discernment I need to avoid the snare of the fowler and walk in the fullness of God's peace. In Jesus Name Amen!

SETTING EXPECTATIONS

In the days, weeks and months to come, you should:

- Cultivate an awareness of your innermost being.
- In big decisions and small ones, learn to pause, step away, and check your spirit for a green, red or yellow light.
- Operate in discernment in all things. Bounce what you're feeling off of a trusted spiritual leader to test your senses.
- Through the continual *consumption* and *confession* of the Word, allow the eternal truths of God to leak from your head to your heart, that you might walk in *heart faith* not just *head knowledge*.

Feel free to write out further goals, expectations and God encounters in the space below:

_____
_____
_____
_____

STERLING HARRIS

7

CIRCUMSTANCES
CHAPTER SIX ACTIVATION GUIDE

HAPPENINGS THAT SPEAK

Unlike the *inward* witness of the previous chapter, circumstances could be considered the *outward* witness in our relationship with God. They are the external events, signs, situations and actions that agree with God's Word, nature, character and voice. Think of God speaking through circumstances as *golden breadcrumbs* from heaven that clue us in on the path God has for us. Circumstances can *display* what God is saying as well as *confirm* what God is saying. Seeing God's fingerprints on a situation by examining the events that unfold has continually helped me recognize His activity.

In Mark 4, we see the disciples in a boat with Jesus. As they are crossing the lake, a massive storm hits them. Jesus is asleep while the disciples are panicking. They wake Jesus and cry out, "Don't you care that we are dying here!?" The Bible does not record that Jesus responded *verbally* at all. It simply says, "He got up, rebuked the wind and said to the waves, 'Quiet! Be still!'

Then the wind died down and it was completely calm" (Mark 4:39 NIV). Jesus responded with *action* instead of words, in this case. The Old Testament reinforces this and says, "You answer us with awesome and righteous *deeds*" (Psalm 65:5 NIV emphasis added). Notice the word *deeds*. In other words, God *responds* to us with *action*. Sometimes we are waiting for a verbal or visual answer in prayer, when God would rather answer by altering circumstances and demonstrating His voice outwardly in your life.

I want to be clear, not *everything* that happens is God will in your life. Don't make the mistake of thinking that when something awful takes place, it was God who instigated it and is trying to speak something to you through it. Recognizing where circumstances come from is key, because they all have their origin in a varied combination of 4 activities:

1. GOD: God can cause circumstances to unfold and play out according to His will in order to better us and grow us. His goal is always to call us into a deeper relational connection with Himself.
2. OUR CHOICES: You and I have the ability to make choices that can either cause death or life in our midst. (See Deuteronomy 30:19.)
3. THE ENEMY: Satan wants to kill, steal and destroy in your midst. He uses unforgiveness, pride, anger, shame, fear, worry, sickness, lust, unbelief, doubt, guilt, sin, isolation and the world system.
4. OTHER'S CHOICES: For better or worse, the behavior of those around us can impact our circumstances greatly.

Circumstances have diverse reasons for playing out the way

they do. As a result, we must *learn to discern* when it is God who is crafting the situation and injecting His voice into it. For example, God will not cause circumstances to occur in order to speak to you if those circumstances go against His nature, character and Word. God will not cause you to sin or cause someone to sin against you, in order to teach you or speak something to you. However, He will use other everyday situations to communicate. I have seen Him use billboards, conversations, street signs, nature, writing on 18-wheelers, answered prayers of all kinds and even people's T-shirts to speak or confirm things I have been asking God about.

Not only that, but God will often speak to me through the time of day or numbers I see in everyday life. Biblically, the number seven stands for completion and the number three represents resurrection, to give a couple of examples. At times, I may see a number that strikes a chord in me and points me to a greater truth. God is constantly sprinkling His voice throughout our day—we can't afford to miss it! Here's why I say that: when we live lives that are aware of God's activity and in a place of gratitude toward His voice, it sets us up to see and hear more of it. Being a good steward means *honoring* what you currently have. We steward God's activity in our day-to-day lives by recognizing and honoring it. For a more in-depth testimony of God speaking through numbers and circumstances, read the story beginning on page 197 of *How to Hear God*.

Circumstances have often been a place of anxiety and confusion for so many. Humanity obsesses over past, present and future circumstances without seeing Jesus in the midst of it all. I used to struggle with projecting myself into future circumstances and it left me feeling anxious, stressed, worried and unfocused. Some call this *future tripping* but I used to call it my everyday life. For years, I struggled to sleep, because my mind would race considering how future events would unfold and what my role would be in them. I eventually learned to give these things to the Lord and began focusing on Him and His role in circumstances—past, present and future.

God wants to redeem our circumstances so that we see them as a hub of His activity. Learn to assess situations by the Holy Spirit. Paul said, "So from now on we regard no one from a worldly point of view. Though we once regarded Christ in this way, we do so no longer" (2 Corinthians 5:16 NIV). In that same way, we don't assess our circumstances in a worldly way or according to the flesh. We look for God's voice, confirmation and leading, which will guide us into our destiny, plan and purpose!

THE **NON-NEGOTIABLES**

- God is deeply connected to our circumstances and *loves* to speak through them.
- We must learn to discern when circumstantial happenings are from God, from other sources or a combination of the four activities.
- To steward God's voice well, we must be *alert* to Him speaking through numbers, times of day, phrases, billboards, situations, and other *outward* events.
- Situations in life should be viewed through the lens of Christ. In so doing, you will redeem circumstances as a place of peace and guidance, not as a place of anxiety and turmoil.

REFLECTION QUESTIONS

God is a Coordinator, Conductor and Confirmation Specialist. (See page 183.) Pray, Ask and Listen: Are there events or circumstances unfolding in your life that God is speaking through? Do an inventory of your current-life situation and write down the breadcrumbs of His voice that you are aware of:

_____
_____
_____
_____
_____
_____

If the enemy can reduce the impact of God's voice in your life from 100 percent to 50k percent, he has seriously wounded your intimacy with God and effectiveness in this world. (See page 190.) Pray, Ask and Listen: Has God's voice, specifically as it pertains to circumstances, been limited? Write out a plan to make the most of all aspects of God's voice in your daily circumstances:

_____
_____
_____
_____
_____
_____

One of the biggest pitfalls in hearing from God is fighting His voice in your head with your intellect and your logical mind. (See page 199.) Have you done this? If so, what did it cost you? What steps can you take moving ahead to cling to His voice by faith, and shake off the doubts that come with mere mental reasoning?

_____
_____
_____
_____
_____
_____

ACTIVATION DECREE

I decree and declare that I will be quickened to seeing God's voice at play in my day-to-day circumstances. I will have eyes to see the voice of the Lord involved in my seemingly mundane routines. May revelation and understanding flow, as sensitivity to the outward expressions of God increases in my life! In Jesus Name Amen!

SETTING **EXPECTATIONS**

In the days, weeks and months to come, you should:

- Keep in mind the four activities we covered when viewing circumstances and ask God for help in discerning what combination of activities are at work.
- No longer view circumstances as events separate from God. Instead, explore the ways in which He may be communicating in the midst of them.
- Ask God to show you numbers, markers, times of day and so forth that may be significant signs and indicators in your journey ahead.
- When envisioning the future, do so hand-in-hand with Jesus.
- Ask God to respond to your desires with *action* and *deeds*. Take note of the circumstantial shifts that follow.

Feel free to write out further goals, expectations and God experiences in the space on the following page:

STERLING HARRIS

> 8
>
> # THE CHURCH AND OTHER PEOPLE
> CHAPTER SEVEN ACTIVATION GUIDE

THE VOICE THROUGH VESSELS

The Church can be defined in two ways. First, the Church is made up of *every single* born again believer in Jesus Christ. Second, the Church is defined as the local assembly of the Church family that you gather with weekly. You will see the Church *differently* when you realize that God speaks through it *consistently*. The body of Christ is a vessel for the voice of the Lord that we should tap into! Perhaps you have listened to a sermon and the preacher said something that felt as though it was directed to you. Often, when I speak, I'll feel myself being inspired to say things that weren't in my notes or part of my preparation. When this happens, I know that God is dealing with people in the congregation and, often, folks will come up afterward revealing how much it spoke to them personally.

God uses preachers and teachers to convey His *general gospel* message as well as His *specific* messages. It's one of the many rich benefits of plugging into a local Church family. Many avoid

Church like the plague because of past experiences with hurt, confusion, abuse or false teaching. People sadly vow to never step foot into a Church again because they have seen hypocrisy and double standards. Yet the Bible urges us, "Let us not give up the habit of meeting together, as some are doing. Instead, let us encourage one another all the more" (Hebrews 10:25 GNT).

So, with that said, there are hypocrites and manipulators in the Church. Yet these people also exist everywhere else we go on a daily basis. You don't stop going to the grocery store or to your job because hypocritical people are there, do you? I want to encourage you to be part of a local Church congregation, where you can build community and healthy relationships with other followers of Jesus! Connect yourself to a local Bible-believing Church in your area that welcomes God's love, voice, presence and the Holy Spirit. Perhaps you're new to all this or you just moved and haven't settled into a local gathering yet. No worries—simply pray, listen and allow the Holy Spirit to lead you to a Church family that is right for you.

Beyond hearing God's voice in a *corporate* setting, like sitting under the teaching from a pastor, God speaks on an *individual* level through His people. The Bible makes it clear that having leaders in your life to provide counsel is crucial. (See Proverbs 11:14.) For me, I have trusted leaders in my life who have room to speak into me and my family. I give them permission and authority to be transparent and loving with me regarding what they see in my life, either positive *or negative*. As you identify these people in your own life, allow them to be open and honest when they give you feedback. Be vulnerable and allow them to share what they sense God might be saying to you. It is a good idea to have several accountability partners to share with relationally who can point out God's activity and voice in your life.

Sometimes, God uses complete strangers to speak to you. You could call them prophetic words, inspired words, anointed encouragements and so forth, but at the end of the day, it's simply a person relaying what they feel God is saying to you. It could be in a formal Church environment or even in a more casual space like a coffee shop or small group. As I've expressed in this book, it *all* has to agree with the Word of God, which is our standard. If it counters God's Word and God's nature, throw it out like last week's leftover sushi!

One of my favorite places to hear God is in the normal flow of life and conversations. I call them *anointed conversations*. This happens when you invite God into your talks with other people by praying, before and during the conversations, for the Holy Spirit to guide your words and heart. It also helps to pray that God would open up their hearts to receive the words God has given you and open your heart to receive from them in a way that honors them and God. I have seen this kind of prayer tactic blaze a trail of favor for myself and others. Anointed conversations have led to the restoration and healing of relationships between family, friends and coworkers.

If God speaks through His Church, and you are a believer, then it must mean that God wants to speak through *you!* You have likely "had someone on your heart" at times in the past. Perhaps the reoccurring thought of a person comes to mind over the course of a few days. Maybe you have a burden to pray for them. When this happens, I would encourage you to press into this and see what God might want to say to them. A God-inspired word of encouragement for them might just be on the other side of your obedience. Inquire of God with questions like:

- *Father God, what's one thing that You want me to share with this person?*
- *Jesus, how do You see them?*
- *Holy Spirit, what do You love about them?*

As you ask God about His heart for them, listen, then write down and speak out what He tells you and shows you. The transformation you will see in your heart, life and in those around you, such as your spouse, kids and coworkers, will be amazing! The legacy of love you live out has the power to impact so many people around you for generations to come. I have witnessed countless breakthroughs in my own personal life and in the lives of others who have intentionally put this into practice. As God gives you a word, ask Him for the boldness you need to deliver it to that person at the right time and in the right spirit.

Hearing God for other people can be one of the most exciting aspects of your Christian life. Don't neglect it! You don't have to be a prophet, nor should you be prophesying who the person should marry or that they should sell their home and move to Africa. Simple words of encouragement and insight from the heart of God will go a long way! Call out the gifts, abilities and talents you see in them. Don't put pressure on yourself to conjure up a deep revelation. Simply let God speak and relay it accordingly. Whether God is using you or using someone else, remember to be watchful, expectant and discerning of how He uses people to speak love, guidance, correction and encouragement into your life and heart!

THE **NON-NEGOTIABLES**

- From Genesis to Revelation, and from the early Church to our modern era, God speaks *through* and *to* His people.
- Being *wounded* by the Church is no reason to *forsake* the Church.
- One role of a trusted leader is to hold you accountable and to have the freedom to share what they feel God is saying in your life.
- As believers, we have a duty to remain open to being used by God to share His voice with other people.

REFLECTION QUESTIONS

Pray, Ask and Listen: Have you been wounded by the Church? If so, you aren't the first. (See page 206.) Sometimes, we may still attend church after being hurt, but we don't plug in or engage with our brothers and sisters. If God shows you some Church hurts, repent for allowing them to take root in your heart and forgive the organization, people and God. Write out some *practical* steps you can take to maximize your Church life to be an effective carrier of God's presence and voice.

_____
_____
_____
_____
_____
_____

Pray, Ask and Listen: Is there a person, people or a group of people heavy on your heart? As you ask God about His heart for them, listen then write down and speak out what He tells you and shows you. (See page 205.) Also, write out the proper motivation behind sharing this word with them.

_____
_____
_____
_____
_____
_____

Are there leaders in your life to hold you accountable and to give you prophetic wisdom? If not, pray and ask God to highlight some godly people in your life who you can be in godly connection with. It's important that you have them. (See page 201.) In the space provided, identify these leaders. Then call or meet with them and ask them what they are seeing for your life. Write out their response.

_____
_____
_____
_____
_____
_____

ACTIVATION DECREE

I decree and declare that divine alignment will take place in my life. I will be brought near to people who will be as the voice of God to me. May I also be as the voice of God to my generation! I speak anointed conversations, revelation, encouragement and wisdom over my life! In Jesus Name Amen!

SETTING EXPECTATIONS

In the days, weeks and months to come, you should:

- If you haven't already, plug into a local Church. If you already have, *maximize* the place where you are and *serve* gladly.
- Prayerfully identity leaders in your life who can keep you *accountable* and speak into your life.
- Consciously listen for what God is saying to those in your midst. If you get a word, *don't hesitate* to share!
- Ask God to set you up in *anointed conversations* and expect them to manifest in your life.

Feel free to write out further goals, expectations and God experiences in the space below:

_____
_____
_____
_____
_____
_____
_____

STERLING HARRIS

> 9
>
> # DREAMS AND VISIONS
> CHAPTER EIGHT ACTIVATION GUIDE

SEEING THE UNSEEN

God likes to talk through dreams and visions. About a third of the Bible was written through accounts of dreams and visions from God. These experiences can be a warning, confirmation, imparted wisdom, correction, teaching, encouragement or other forms of guidance. Before getting too deep into this, let me be clear—some dreams are *just* dreams. However, more often than people realize, dreams can have a deeper meaning from God, particularly when you have surrendered your dream life to the Lord by asking Him to visit you in the night season.

A dream is something you will generally have while you are asleep. A vision is something you generally see in your mind while you are awake *or* they can take place while you are asleep. I would describe visions while asleep as *vivid dreams.* The scriptural basis for this form of divine communication is quite evident. We see that Joseph was continually experiencing powerful dreams from the Lord that positioned him for great increase. Daniel was gifted with the ability to interpret dreams for others. Even Job said, "In a dream, in a vision of the night, when deep sleep falls upon men, while slumbering on their beds, then He opens the ears of men, and seals their instruction" (Job 33:15-16).

When I began to see such things and welcome them into my life, dreams and visions started to culture my life and heart, because I finally recognized God was actually communicating with me through them and I stopped dismissing them as just random, weird or strange dreams. In order to decipher whether or not your dream is from the Lord, we have to see the three distinct origins of dreams:

1. GOD: A dream from God is His communication with us as we sleep, giving us the message or messages we need for a particular situation or season.
2. THE SOUL: A dream caused by our soul takes place when our mind, will, emotions and even flesh construct a dream. For example, a soulish dream is often self-centered and full of self-promotion. It could also be more benign and simply a regurgitation of something you did the day before.
3. DEMONIC DREAMS: These are perverse dreams that might be riddled with sin, adultery, fear, confusion or worse. These dreams might more accurately be categorized as nightmares or night terrors. The blood and name of Jesus are your best friends when dealing with these issues. Submit your dream life to God! Even when the enemy gives you a dream, pay attention, because he will expose his plan! Then you are able to pray the opposite of what

the enemy is trying to do in your life and heart. Another technique is praying in tongues to combat demonic dreams and thoughts.

Talk to God about your dreams. As you do, you may experience an inward knowledge that will reveal a deeper meaning and interpretation of the dream or vision. The Holy Spirit will enable you to decipher the origin and meaning of the dream. Regarding dream interpretation, Joseph said, "Do not interpretations belong to God?" (Genesis 40:8 NIV). He is the one who provides the meaning, yet we must partner with His methods.

One of the best ways to begin to see this area of your life flourish is through dream journaling. I encourage you to keep a notebook on your nightstand or designate a note on your phone to record your experiences in the dream world. When you awake, either in the morning or in the middle of the night, write down the dream you feel was significant. If you wait, you might forget it, and if you forget it, you won't benefit from it. Writing it down allows you to go back and view the record of God's activity throughout the eb and flow of your life. If you are married, it is wise to let your spouse know what you are doing and encourage them to do the same thing with their dreams.

Learn to value this avenue for hearing the voice of God. Some of the ways we can practically value dreams are to write them down, capture them on the voice recorder or talk-to-text on your phone, pray about them, ask God to tell you and show you the meaning of the dream and research and study biblical dream symbols and meanings to develop your understanding of dreams. God is not trying to make this process difficult. Oftentimes, people complicate things God made to be simple. The late John Paul Jackson has great resources on this subject. In fact, his *Dream Dictionary* on his website has a treasure of information to help you decode and decipher what God is saying to you in the night seasons.

Dreams are often filled with figurative pictures that point to things going on in your life. Puns, for instance, are often used. The *sun,* in a dream, can often be a reference to Jesus, the *Son* of God. If a dream is dimly lit or taking place at night, God might be revealing that something in your life is bringing in darkness. Another common pattern God uses in dreams is in the people who show up in them. Often, God is using their character traits, who they represent in your personal life or God may be prompting you to look up the actual meaning of their name in order to convey a symbolic and metaphorical message to you.

The Lord uses object lessons and symbols to illustrate a desired message to us. The interpretation of dreams and visions is, in fact, the *first* spiritual gift I ever prayerfully asked God for, and, like the good Father He is, it was His pleasure to give it to me. I have been honing that gift for a number of years and it continues to grow in me. God will do the same for you! As I developed in this area, here are a few questions I've often used to help in my dream journey:

1. Lord, what does this part of my dream mean?
2. Jesus, what are You saying to me in this dream?
3. Holy Spirit, what do You want me to do in response to this dream?

Bear in mind, the treasure hunt *always* needs to be guided by the Holy Spirit, by prayerfully asking God to highlight and make known the meaning of the dream. The enemy knows the power of dreams and wants to dissuade you from getting the most out of them. Be faithful to journal and explore with Jesus. I have been deeply impacted by this practice. If you would like a more in-depth look at examples and encounters I've experienced in this arena, I encourage you to read the testimonies beginning on page 223 of *How to Hear God*.

Similar to a dream, a vision is a perception, often within your imagination, that allows you to see a mental picture, video, scene or symbol that relates to what God is trying to get across to you. You may experience a vision in which the real world in front of you disappears and suddenly you only see a flash of what God is revealing to you. Some describe this as an "open vision." This takes place when your eyes are open yet you are not seeing the natural world in front of you—you are seeing something God is superimposing onto your vision. Other times, you may have your eyes closed and encounter an image that God brings into your mind.

This takes place when your eyes are open and you may or may not be seeing the natural world in front of you—you are seeing something God is superimposing onto your vision like a faint hologram. Whether it's a dream, a vision or an optic experience that you can't define, I encourage you to make a habit of journaling it and mulling it over in prayer. As you do, you will find *rich* and *insightful* messages from the Lord that you would have missed otherwise.

THE **NON-NEGOTIABLES**

- To God, communicating via dreams and visions is normal. Well over 20 percent of the Bible was written from inspirations given in dreams or visions.
- Dreams have one of three origins: God, the soul and the enemy.
- Journaling and praying over your dream life will cause increase and clarity in this area.
- It's a good idea to research and discover dream symbolism to fully grasp the significance and meaning of a dream.

REFLECTION QUESTIONS

God seals instruction in our hearts through dreams. (See page 214.) Pray, Ask and Listen: Are there dreams you have had in the past that have a deeper meaning and instruction that you've not yet tapped into? Consider impactful dreams you have had and write out any interpretation that God gives you for them.

_____
_____
_____
_____
_____
_____

Dreams can come from God, your soul or even the demonic realm. (See page 214.) Specifically, what are key indicators of each? How can you tell if a dream *did not* come from the Lord?

_____
_____
_____
_____
_____
_____

Dreams often contain symbolism that points to greater truth. (See page 217.) Are there recurring symbols, people, patterns or events that you see in your dreams? Write them out. Then look up their meaning and piece together the puzzle of what God might be saying to you.

_____
_____
_____
_____
_____
_____

ACTIVATION DECREE

I decree and declare that my night seasons will be filled and flooded with the voice of God. May I be enlightened with interpretations, keys, and revelations as I slumber. I rebuke unrest, sleeplessness, nightmares and insomnia in Jesus' name, and declare that my nights belong to God alone, from this day forward! Amen!

SETTING **EXPECTATIONS**

In the days, weeks and months to come, you should:

- Dedicate your dream life to God and ask Him to open up your dreams to experience His voice. (Sample prayer found on page 215.)
- Prepare to write out, document your dreams and talk them over with God whenever they occur.
- Research symbols, biblical examples and hidden meanings that often occur in dream patterns.
- Pursue the interpretation to dreams you have had in the past that you might have overlooked.

Feel free to write out further goals, expectations and God encounters in the space below:

_____
_____
_____
_____
_____
_____
_____
_____
_____
_____
_____
_____

10

CHRISTIAN MUSIC AND WORSHIP
CHAPTER NINE ACTIVATION GUIDE

MUSIC WITH A MESSAGE

The lyrics of a song can become a message from God when He breathes on it. Have you experienced a worship song or Christian music speaking to your heart in a personal way? That is the voice of God! Throughout the Bible, we see God's emphasis on music, singing, dancing, instruments and songs. David was so passionate about this that he actually invented instruments for His worship with God. (See Amos 6:5.)

Music and the voice of God are so intertwined that the biggest book of the Bible is a song book (Psalms). The psalms are a beautiful collection of writings, all inspired by God's voice, that encourage us to worship and praise our King. There are times when I am praying when I turn on some music and, as I am asking God a question or as I am talking to Him, my ear seems to tune into the song at just the right moment and it seems as if God is speaking directly to my heart through the song lyrics. I've heard many people share of experiencing similar things. God will grab hold of words or phrases within a song and cause them to stand out to you! He does this in the same manner that He does with a sermon or teaching.

Not only does God speak through the words of a song but He also speaks through the *atmosphere* that the song creates. There have been songs I have heard numerous times before, but when they are played at certain times, I am moved within my heart by the Holy Spirit in a powerful way, often tearing up and weeping as the song seems to take on new meaning at that moment in time. This is God speaking to and touching us with His tangible presence. You may experience this same phenomenon when reading your Bible.

Worship itself draws you closer to God relationally, which positions you to hear from Him more clearly. You don't have to be a good singer or a talented musician to worship Jesus effectively. Simply lay your heart out before Him. Think about how good it feels when someone you love speaks words of gratitude of how thankful they are for you and how much you mean to them. Worship is you ministering to and caring for God's heart, which, in turn, transforms and blesses your heart in the process.

David was so passionate about the Lord that He expressed His worship in unusual ways at times. Once, he danced through the streets in his undergarments instead of his royal clothes and kingly robe in celebration! He shamelessly let go of all reservations and committed himself to glorifying God. Many struggle to express themselves in worship due to fear of what others might think. I want to encourage you to let go of your self-consciousness and magnify Jesus with all of your being.

I remember the very moment God began to shift my thinking in this. I was standing in Church one day and I wanted to raise both of my hands but I was struggling in my inner dialogue: *Am I going to look foolish to others around me? Am I just drawing attention to myself? Am I really feeling the song that much? God would be unhappy with me. I am not that holy and have no right to worship God like that. I would be a hypocrite if I do that.* Right then and there, the Spirit of God spoke to me in the form of a flowing thought. God said, "Sterling, you were the hype-guy for your football team. You were the person always dancing in the club and wanted to be the life of the party. You get so into football and the things of the world but you want to hold back when it comes to worshipping and loving Me?"

Immediately, video clips began to play in my mind of how I used to hold back in my worship of God in Church and when I listened to Christian music, when, at the same time, I saw myself getting all pumped up about secular rap, country and rock music. I saw myself jumping around before football practice and games, getting the other players hyped up as I literally went wild during a game emotionally. God showed me how I yelled and jumped around watching the playoffs in football and basketball on TV. The last set of visions featured me in nightclub hotspots, singing along with the songs and dancing in the VIP section like I was in the latest rap video. At that point, the Holy Spirit rose up within me and a boldness came over me. I declared, "No more!" I am going to dance, sing, praise and worship God with a higher degree of boldness and joy than I had for any sporting event, nightclub or hit secular non-Christian song! Right then, I raised both of my hands and began to jump up and down and I decided to be a joyous child before the Lord, worshiping Him with all that I am in childlike faith! That moment changed my life forever.

Let me say, if you demonstrate more passion, joy and energy for sports or your favorite secular song than you do Jesus, you might want to take a look at what is going on in your heart.

Music is a huge part of our culture and some of us spend hours a day listening to it. Whether in the car, in the shower or at the gym, most people have music playing throughout their day. It is important to realize that what you continually allow to come into your heart will eventually affect your thoughts, words and actions. Why does this matter? Because it will eventually come out of your heart and manifest itself in your life. The more words filled with faith, hope, love and righteousness that you put into your heart on a daily basis, the more of those same things will come out in the thoughts you think, in the things you say and in the daily choices you make. Choose to take in wholesome, faith-filled music and enjoy the benefits of it.

THE **NON-NEGOTIABLES**

- Songs can *carry* God's messages into your ears and heart.
- The single biggest book of God's voice (the Psalms) is a collection of songs and worship.
- Self-consciousness in worship will rob us of our full expression of love to God.
- We internalize and regurgitate what we continually fill up on. Therefore, a healthy diet of Christ-centered music is more than wise.

REFLECTION QUESTIONS

Anointed lyrics can penetrate our hearts and give us the Rhema Word of God. (See page 229.) Are there certain songs that have spoken to you in the past? List them below. Describe what you sense God has communicated to you through them.

_____
_____
_____
_____
_____
_____

God wants you to have a vibrant, passionate love-relationship with Him. (See page 233.) In the space provided, write out a song to Him. You don't have to be a talented songwriter to do this. From a place of gratitude, simply put together lyrics, phrases, or a chorus that the Holy

Spirit gives you. Go ahead! I double dare you to have some fun doing this!

___

When the enemy is attacking, there is no better time to worship. (See page 232.) What have been your experiences in worshipping in the midst of the storm? What role has continual thanksgiving played in your Christian walk?

___

ACTIVATION DECREE

I decree and declare that the melodies of heaven will fill my being. May I hear the voice of God in the form of a song. Hymns, poems, psalms and songs are mine to sing out. A life of praise and gratitude is now mine! In Jesus Name Amen!

SETTING **EXPECTATIONS**

In the days, weeks and months to come, you should:

- Avail yourself to a *diverse* array of Christian music and worship songs.
- Take note of the ways in which God speaks to you through music, whether in word or in atmosphere.
- Step out in faith and express your worship to God the way you feel led and free from self-consciousness.
- Let unique songs, phrases and melodies flow from your heart throughout your day.

Feel free to write out further goals, expectations and God experiences in the space below:

11

CREATION
CHAPTER TEN ACTIVATION GUIDE

THE EARTH DECLARES

The order, art and design of the earth all declare the voice of the Lord in magnificent ways. Paul said, "Ever since God created the world, His invisible qualities, both His eternal power and His divine nature, have been clearly seen; they are perceived in the things that God has made" (Romans 1:20 GNT). People have *perceived* God through His creation since the beginning of time. However, many of us do not recognize what creation *truly* means for God's people.

God spoke creation into existence. (See Genesis 1.) Everything we see is the result of God speaking, yet it doesn't stop there. The actual creation that exists *because* of the voice of God also exists to *perpetuate* the voice of God. The intricate beauty of a flower speaks of God's excellence and taste. The perfect design of a sunset speaks of His loving artistry. God, in His generosity and provision, knew that we would need food, which He provided, but He also gave us the ability to taste, experience texture, flavor and so forth. We can clearly see that creation is a love language. The care that went into the world around us is a loud declaration from the mouth of God, saying, "I love you."

Have you ever found yourself in a place of despair or trapped in your own thoughts when, suddenly, you notice the colorful fall leaves or a fragrant aroma that alleviates the troubles of your day? Perhaps a trip to the ocean is like therapy to your soul. Maybe the song of a bird or a glimpse of a rainbow brings a certain peace to your heart. God has spoken through creation and provided generous benefits through it. He is constantly speaking through what He has made!

Consider this, how did God tell Noah He would remind him of His covenant? Through a rainbow. What did Jesus say was one of the signs of the end times? Earthquakes. (See Matthew 24.) To be even more literal, God spoke through a donkey in the Scriptures. (See Numbers 22.) God actually kickstarted the great prophet Jeremiah's prophetic ministry by speaking to Him about the symbolism of an almond tree!

Many of the whispers of Heaven are found out in nature. As I explain in chapter 8 of *How to Hear God*, the Lord used a dream of a large flourishing oak tree to explain, encourage and guide me into a huge part of my purpose, destiny and calling in life. From there, I looked for more detail about what God was saying in this particular dream. I researched Scriptures that talked about trees. For example, in Psalm 1:3, it says, "He will be like a tree firmly planted by streams of water, which yields its fruit in its season. And its leaf does not wither; and in whatever he does, he prospers" (ESV).

As I read it, this Scripture agreed with my spirit, meaning I felt a peace in my innermost being that this was part of what God was saying by showing me a tree in my dream. The interpretation God spoke to my heart is this: I am a tree (a person) that is firmly planted by streams of water (symbolic of the Word of God and the Holy Spirit) and I will yield fruit (the fruit of the Holy Spirit and blessings, see Galatians 5:22) through this ministry as He prospers me by His hand. God eventually led us to use the tree from my dreams and visions as part of our ministry logo.

Sometimes, when I see a tree near streams of water or a large mountain with trees near the summit, I sense God using nature to speak to my heart, encouraging me to stay the course in my calling to manifest Jesus to the world. God wants to use these types of things to speak to you also! For my wife, God speaks through red cardinals, doves, falcons and butterflies. For you, it may be something totally different. Simply be open and aware of God speaking through anything. Scriptures are filled with passages imploring us to see the beauty of God's splendor, wisdom and majesty in creation.

As I was jogging one day, God spoke to my spirit, meaning I had this flowing thought from the Holy Spirit within me, saying, "Stop for a second. I want to talk to you." It was my heavenly Father! He said, "Do you see these birds, these trees and all the different plant life, wildlife and insects?" I said, "Yes, Lord, I do." He said, "Everything you see glorifies Me. It does exactly what I created it to do. Everything on this earth glorifies Me by its God-given instinct, except you, Sterling." I was convicted and felt a godly sorrow because I knew it was true. God lovingly went on to say, "Humans are the only beings on earth with the power to speak words, the power of freewill and the ability to choose to have a relationship with Me and glorify Me, or not to do so." After that conversation, I was so humbled and began to see God in every part of creation and how He uses it to speak to us about the depths of His glory, power and presence. A simple jog around this beautiful wooded area marked me and changed my heart as I stopped and took in God's creation and the great honor He gives us, as humans, to choose to love Him and have a personal relationship in which the God of the universe comes to live inside of us. God speaks through creation every day! I want to encourage you to tune your heart into the frequency of God's voice and love language as He communicates to you through all of His vast creation!

THE **NON-NEGOTIABLES**

- The *intricate* details of creation displays clearly the caring, provisional nature of God.
- God has *installed* peaceful, comforting and calming elements in nature.
- The Bible is *filled* with accounts of God using natural things in the earth to get His message across.
- Taking the time to stop and enjoy creation will open us to *fine-tuning* our perception of God's voice.

REFLECTION QUESTIONS

God gave us five senses, by which we interact with the physical world around us. (See page 239.) How does this relate to our *spiritual* walk with God? Do we have spiritual senses? What are they and how do we function in them?

_____
_____
_____
_____
_____
_____

I mention in the chapter various animals that mean something spiritual to my wife. (See page 241.) Are there animals, trees, types of flowers or something in nature that you feel drawn to or tend to notice often? What symbolism do they have and what do you sense God is communicating to you through nature?

God lovingly corrected me when He spoke to me about how creation was glorifying Him but I was choosing not to in some areas of my life. (See page 241.) Pray, Ask and Listen: Have you found yourself in this place? How can you remedy this? List actionable steps to take in the space provided.

ACTIVATION DECREE

I decree and declare that my eyes, ears, and senses will be given a new sensitivity to stop and appreciate the creation that God has put in front of me. Lord, thank You for speaking prophetically to me through the natural world. I pray that I would be awakened to the beauty of God's nature by beholding the beauty of created nature, from this moment forward! In Jesus Name Amen!

SETTING **EXPECTATIONS**

In the days, weeks and months to come, you should:

- Spend time outside, beholding the *beauty* of what God has made.
- Study the many biblical accounts of the prophetic symbolism and significance that nature carries.
- Seek to glorify Jesus with total, singular focus, in the same way that creation does.
- Tune the frequency of your heart to the language God uses when communicating through His vast creation.

Feel free to write out further goals, expectations and God encounters in the space below:

12

THE DEMONSTRATION OF GOD'S LOVE AND POWER (PART 1)
CHAPTER ELEVEN ACTIVATION GUIDE

DIVINITY ON DISPLAY

Intimacy with Jesus allows us to hear His voice. His voice and Word give us our sense of *identity*—we begin to know who we are. When this occurs, we step into a place of *influence*, which is our inheritance. *Intimacy, identity* and *influence* are the genuine goals of this book and the bedrock of a solid Christian life. One of the primary reasons that hearing God is so important is because it enables us to give His voice away to someone else. Are there times when God speaks things to you, and *you only*, for your benefit? Sure! But so often, He speaks things *to* you to get them *through* you. You cannot give out what you don't possess. If you are possessed by the love of the Father, the grace of Jesus and the power of the Holy Spirit, then what is within you will come out of you on a daily basis.

Demonstrating God's love and power to the world around us should be done *in that order.* We aren't called to attempt to demonstrate God's power without God's love. Love is the motivation and fuel behind all that we do. We are called to live in a daily *love* relationship with God, allowing Him to love us by opening our hearts to receive His unconditional love consistently. In this, we find our identity in knowing Him as we love and value ourselves as His sons and daughters. Out of that intimate love exchange and overflow, we are then empowered to love those around us.

Our great role model in this is Jesus, Himself. By His love, He was able to transform the people whom others, especially the religious people of that time, deemed as unreachable and of no value. Jesus always kept His love on, shining it toward people. He molded and shaped people's hearts with the love, power and goodness of God the Father! Paul said, "The only thing that matters is faith working through love" (Galatians 5:6 NET). The question we have to ask is: How did Jesus love others? The ways are innumerable, but here is a short list:

- He valued people
- He listened to people
- He challenged people
- He spoke God's truth to people
- He encouraged people
- He modeled how to live in relationship with the Father
- He sacrificially laid down His life for humanity

Beyond that, He operated in the gifts of the Holy Spirit, healed the sick, cast out demons, performed miracles, prophesied over people, operated in words of knowledge, cleansed those with leprosy, raised the dead and preached the truth of the gospel to all who would listen. He was often moved with compassion and expressed the deepest levels of empathy possible. The beautiful thing about this holy standard is that we also have been commissioned to *go* and do likewise.

The Scriptures say, "And Jesus said to them, 'Go into all the world and preach the gospel to all creation. ...These signs will accompany those who have believed: in My name they will cast out demons, they will speak in new tongues; they will pick up serpents, and if they drink anything deadly, it will not hurt them; they will lay hands on the sick, and they will get well'" (Mark 16:15,17-18 AMP). At this moment, what we call *the great commission,* Christ's commission, became our mission. His tasks on earth became ours. His motivation became ours.

We have been equipped with the same mandate, motivation and methods, to carry out the works of Christ. Notice the passage in Mark says these *signs* will accompany us as believers! We don't follow signs; signs follow us. We have been equipped to release the love and power of the kingdom. Saying, "I believe in God" is not enough. We have to step into our full identity. What does this look like? It looks like saying what Jesus *said* and doing what Jesus *did.*

If you are a believer, draw a circle around where you're standing. Revival starts within that circle, within your own heart, then your home, and then it spreads to the world around you. This doesn't mean that you must have a massive ministry platform or preach crusades to millions. It means being emotionally present and actively listening to your spouse, kids, family, friends and others. It means being alert and ready to respond with Christ's love and power in any given moment.

I can recall a time when I had the chance to demonstrate the love and power of Jesus in a somewhat unexpected way. I was heading to the grocery store for a quick trip at around 11 pm. As I approached the entrance, I saw two young men sitting outside, and it was as if God highlighted them to me. I felt compelled to help them. They approached me and said that they were hungry and wanted something to eat. I said, "Well, come into the store with me and I will buy you both some food." As we went through the store grabbing food off of the shelves for them, I asked them about their situation and made it clear that I valued what they were saying. It became obvious that they desperately needed life transformation.

I broke the ice and said, "Do you have a relationship with Jesus Christ?" They both stated, "No, I am not religious, but I respect all religions." I said, "Good, I am not religious either. I have a spiritual love relationship with Jesus Christ." They seemed puzzled at my answer. I said, "I am in love with Jesus, meaning I have a daily relationship with God in which I experience His love and know Him personally. He loves you and wants to have an intimate relationship with you too. God, through Jesus Christ, wants to give you His love, acceptance, understanding, joy, peace and righteousness. Would you like to have more of those things in your life?"

This is a great tool because everyone wants more of these things! From there, I began sharing my testimony with them. I was not preaching *at them* but sharing God's love *with them.* You don't have to be able to quote a ton of Scripture or give a deep theological explanation. Simply sharing your story and the simple gospel, *in love*, is plenty. That night, I led them in a *prayer of salvation*. They confessed that Jesus is Lord and surrendered their lives to Him. Not only that, but when we opened our eyes after the prayer, I learned of another miracle. One of the young men shared that he was shocked that when he opened his eyes something physically had changed. He was amazed and looked over at his friend and said, "Bro, do you know how I have been complaining the last couple of days, about my eyes being foggy because my contacts scratched my corneas?" His friend responded inquisitively, "Yeah, what's up?" He continued, "Bro, I can see clearly now. My eyes are totally healed!" I began to laugh at the goodness of God and the phrase of a song joyfully rose out of my heart. I began to sing the song, "I can see clearly now, the rain is gone!" (Johnny Nash)

Experiencing these sorts of encounters is not complicated. I often ask people direct questions to get the ball rolling, such as, "Do you have a relationship with Jesus? How is your relationship with Jesus? On a scale of 1 to 10, with 10 being *on fire for Jesus* and 1 being born again but not knowing much else, where do you find yourself?" I encourage them that God wants a deeper relationship with all of us. Some people think we can only evangelize the lost, yet there is plenty of room to share with and encourage those who are already saved but need encouragement! Many of the people Jesus ministered to already knew Him.

Don't let the fear of rejection, the fear of people and fear of judgment stop you from being the Jesus people need to see and experience in this world on a daily basis! Rejection will happen. While we generally share success stories in the pulpit and in books, they aren't always the case. Just remember that people are not rejecting *you* personally. They're saying *no* to the message. Continue to love them and sow seeds of grace. As you do your part, rest assured, God will do His.

THE NON-NEGOTIABLES

- *Intimacy, identity* and *influence* are the prizes and goals of the Christian faith.
- Christ's *mandate, motivation* and *methods* have become ours also, because of the great commission in Mark 16.
- Revival starts with you. We are not called to be Christians *in name only* but also in *action*.
- The fear of rejection has hindered many. God's will is for us to *push past* this barrier and step into our callings as influencers.

REFLECTION QUESTIONS

Jesus was in constant communication with the Father, which empowered Him to minister to those in His day. (See page 246.) We are to follow the same model. What are the negative consequences of attempting to demonstrate God's kingdom without having intimacy with God Himself?

_____
_____
_____
_____
_____
_____

Our purpose as believers is to manifest God's love to those around us especially those closest to us. (See page 245.) Pray, Ask and Listen: Specifically, what would this look like for you? Write out a few practical goals for how you can walk this out in the coming weeks.

Who are the groups God has given you to bring the gospel to? Paul was called to the Gentiles. Peter was called to the Jews. Some are called to people in business, education, politics or the mission field. We are all qualified for the sphere God has given us. (See page 259.) Pray, Ask and Listen: For you personally, what does your sphere of influence look like? Are there groups, people, regions, spheres or arenas that have a specific place in your heart?

ACTIVATION DECREE

I decree and declare that opportunities to share the love and power of God will be coming to me soon. I will break past the barrier of fear and boldly proclaim the loving gospel of Jesus to those in front of me. May the intimacy I cultivate in the secret place result in influence in the public place. In Jesus Name Amen!

SETTING **EXPECTATIONS**

In the days, weeks and months to come, you should:

- Step out in faith and share the gospel with and pray for the people God highlights to you within your daily life.
- Refuse the fear of rejection. Allow the Holy Spirit to embolden you like He did the Church in Acts 2.
- Intentionally break the ice and be an influencer among your family, friends and the world around you.
- Let God refine your motivations. Learn to hurt for the hurting world.

Feel free to write out further goals, expectations and God experiences in the space below:

_____
_____
_____
_____
_____
_____
_____
_____
_____
_____
_____

> # 13
>
> # THE DEMONSTRATION OF GOD'S LOVE AND POWER (PART 2)
>
> CHAPTER ELEVEN ACTIVATION GUIDE

DIVINE HEALING

Through divine healing, you can hear God's active voice, sense His activity, as well as experience His supernatural power at work in a tangible way. I want to be clear from the outset of this chapter that healing is *always* the will of God. He did not design us to be sick. Jesus came to destroy all sickness and disease. Everyone who came to Him was healed. If Jesus would have turned away just *one* person or said, "I'm not willing" on just *one* occasion, we would have reason to believe His will to heal wavers. Yet this is *not* the case. He relentlessly healed the masses. Included in His redemptive plan is the promise of healing for all who come to Him. While we don't have the time to comprehensively unpack all of the hundreds of passages in Scripture on healing, I want to provide you with a short list, from both the Old Testament to New, to help you reinforce God's desire to heal.

- Acts 10:38
- Psalm 103:3
- Exodus 15:26
- 1 Peter 2:24
- James 5:14-16
- Mark 1:34

When praying for healing for others, or for yourself, there is often the fear of disappointment or of being judged as weird or fanatical that comes into play. The reality is, as a believer, if you want to see God's power, you have to get over the fear of disappointment and of people rejecting you. At the end of the day, when you offer to pray for people, most of the time, they are not going to turn you down, and most of them won't know what to expect. So even if nothing happens in the naturally seen realm, at the very least, they will simply be blessed by your gesture and will feel noticed, loved and valued. In truth, no matter what happens when you pray, the seed of God's Word and healing power just got planted in their body and is working to heal them from the inside out.

As you step out and pray for others, here are some practical things to keep in mind. First, if you hear of someone who is hurting physically, be encouraged to pray for them. You will see more miracles by simply stepping out any chance you get than you would if you were reserved and cautious. If someone is hurting, simply tell them, "Hey, the Bible says that the prayer of faith heals the sick. Can I pray for you? What do you have to lose?" This helps build faith in the person receiving prayer *and* gives them a biblical understanding as to why you are doing what you are doing.

When I pray for people, I start by asking them to state the level of their pain, on a scale of 1 to 10. This way, if there is a shift in their condition, they can quantify it. If you are going to lay hands on the person, seek their permission first so long as it's an appropriately safe place on their body, like a knee or ankle. As a safety and comfort issue, especially with the opposite gender, you want to ask for permission to place your hand on their shoulder as a point of contact. If they say no or seem uncomfortable with that, it is not a big deal—the power comes in the Word and the blood of Jesus being applied.

Keep the volume of your voice in mind. If you are in the middle of a crowded grocery store, there is no reason to shout like you're going to scare the sickness away. This can scare or embarrass the person. Remember, if they have a negative experience, it may be the last time they accept prayer from someone again. We have to be sensitive. Loud prayers don't mean effective prayers. Pray passionately and in faith but in a normal tone of voice. Jesus has already healed the person. The payment was made at the cross. We are simply stepping out to thank Him for what He has done and receiving His free gift.

Once you have said "amen," ask the person to do something they could not before, or ask them to re-rate the pain. If nothing happened or things are only marginally better for them, ask if you can pray for them again. Jesus prayed for a blind man twice before the full manifestation took place—you can do so too. (See Mark 8.) At the end of the day, if the person doesn't experience the breakthrough that we would like to see, be humble and encourage them by saying, "The Word of God is like a seed. I believe that it will grow and grow to bring about full healing in your body." Encourage them with healing Scriptures and remember to pray for them later. Many times, people who have not been healed on the spot later report that they were completely set free overnight or in the next few days.

Let me share a brief example from my own life to reinforce

these things. At work one day, I saw a coworker walking stiffly. I asked him what was going on. He told me that he had been experiencing severe back pain and a lack of mobility. I asked him about his pain level and he told me it was at an 8 out of 10 and that he could not currently bend over and touch his toes. I said, "Jesus said, 'These signs will follow them that believe, you will lay hands on the sick and they will get well.' Jesus is a healer, can I pray for Him to heal your back?" He said, "Yes, you may." Then I asked him, "What would it look like for you to be healed?" He said if his pain level went down and he could touch his toes without pain then he would know Jesus healed him. I said, "Can I place my hand on the middle of your back and shoulder?" Again, he agreed.

I simply prayed, "Jesus, I thank You that You are a healer. Back, I speak to you, in Jesus' name, and I command you to be healed by the blood of Jesus. Pain, be gone. Back, be healed, in Jesus' name, amen." Then I asked him to check his pain level and range of motion. His pain level went from an 8 to a 4 and he could bend over farther than before. We praised God and celebrated the victory! Then I asked, "Can I pray for you again real quick for *all* the pain to go away?" He nodded yes. I prayed again and asked him to check his back again. It had gone from a pain level of 8 to a 4 to a 1! The Word of God is like a hammer; it keeps hammering away at sickness, illness and disease the more you use it, until the healing is totally received by their bodies. There are times I have prayed as many as four times for a certain person, depending on the circumstances.

Contend for healing and press in. Don't overthink what is happening. Trust God. Healing is like having access to a bank account that's full of money. Healing has already been paid for, thus, we simply make withdrawals on what God has made available. I would encourage you to take a look at the accounts of healings starting on page 270 in *How to Hear God*. By them, I pray you will be given *inspiration* and *insight* to step out in your journey of ministering with Jesus, the Great Physician.

LIVING A PROPHETIC LIFESTYLE

When Paul describes the gifts of the Holy Spirit, he unpacks nine gifts in total. (See 1 Corinthians 12.) Those nine gifts can be divided into three categories and are meant for the entire body of Christ, as we desire them and open ourselves to them:

MANIFESTATION GIFTS

- Faith
- Gifts of healings
- Miracles

REVELATION GIFTS

- Word of knowledge
- Word of wisdom
- Discerning of spirits

SPEAKING/VERBAL GIFTS

- Prophecy
- Tongues
- Interpretation of tongues

These gifts are functions of the Holy Spirit, given as needed to demonstrate the love and power of Christ. We talked previously about healings and miracles, but I would like to hone in on a couple of gifts from the *revelation* and *verbal* categories, specifically, the word of knowledge and the gift of prophecy. A word of knowledge can be described as details, information and knowledge about someone or something that the Holy Spirit communicates to you through supernatural means. We see this at work in the Gospels, where Jesus would know things about people that He couldn't have known in the natural, as in the story of the woman at the well in John 4. A word of knowledge can come in the form of thoughts, mental images, impressions, or inner knowings that show up spontaneously or when requested. Truthfully, a word of knowledge can manifest by any of the methods of hearing God we have discussed in this book.

Chapter 11 of *How to Hear God* contains extensive examples of operating in this gift, however, I will share a brief testimony with you here. One evening, I was spending some time with a young man and I saw a faint hologram-like image of an exclamation mark and a golden pen above the young man's head for just a split second. I got the impression he was a writer and did some form of creative writing. At first, he said, "No, I'm not a writer. I don't really like English." I thought I had missed it. Yet I try to remind myself that just stepping out by faith can have amazing effects on people's lives, and when you do get it wrong, at least you tried. In this case, a few minutes later the young man said, "Hey, it just dawned on me, I write spoken words that are similar to raps. Those are creative writings, I just never thought of them in that way until I was thinking about what you said God showed you!" I laughed and said, "Well God loves your writings and, evidently, He has given you a golden pen to write them with!" We prayed together for God to give him amazing lyrics that would mark and change a generation for God! After we spoke, he even sent me a couple he had written!

Some words of knowledge are more abstract in the way they come like word associations. I was once at a dinner party talking to a lady. As she began to talk about her grown children, I suddenly had a flashback to a friend of mine named Doug. Somehow, I knew within myself that this lady had a child named Doug. I took a leap of faith and said, "Pardon me for interrupting you. This may seem a little odd but I got this thought about my friend Doug and I get the sense God is showing me that it is one of your son's names. Is that true?" She said, "Did I tell you that?" I said, "No, Jesus gave me that name." She began to cry at the sense of God knowing her heart for her son. As it turned out, her son's middle name was Douglas and he had been going through some challenging things in life. I could sense and see God's presence wrapping around her in a big Holy Ghost hug!

A word of knowledge often lends itself to the gift of prophecy. Often, when people hear the word *prophesying*, they think of someone being able to foretell the future or give insight about future events by divine revelation. This does take place, however, prophesying can also be a divine revelation and spiritual insight from God about past and present things as well. The Bible is clear that prophesying is something all Christians can do. (See 1 Corinthians 14:5.) In fact, Paul urged us to go after it! The Word tells us, in 1 Corinthians 14:3, what prophecy should sound like when we hear it from God and how we should deliver it, in love, to the person we are speaking to, "But the person who prophesies speaks to people for their upbuilding, encouragement, and comfort." Put simply, prophecy is an inspired word from God to build up, encourage and comfort another person.

For example, a while back, my brother had some critical business decisions to make and did not know what to do. I said, "Hey bro, lets pray and listen to what the Holy Spirit is saying about your business." In the natural world, it didn't seem like it would matter. However, as we were praying, he and I both received some strategic insight from God that we shared with one another. Then we began praying blessings and prophesying over his business, based on what God showed us, and as we did that by faith, and led by the Holy Spirit, a comfort, encouragement and inner confidence came. He began to put some of the strategic insight that God had given us into action, and less than three weeks later, his business had a huge turn around and his revenues *increased* dramatically.

Entire books could be written, and have been written, on the subject of prophecy. Yet, to distill it to its simplest form, prophecy is just *saying what God says the way He wants you to say it*. It often is accompanied by words of knowledge and special insight. We touched on these things in chapter seven, so I won't belabor the point, but I want to assure you, it is exciting to hear God's voice for yourself and it's just as exciting to hear His voice for someone else. As you grow in these various methods of hearing God, you will become a more effective witness. You will improve as a vessel in your home, in your workplace, in your ministry and in every area of your life.

So many people experience Christianity as a *works-based religion*, in which their success is determined by their behavior, Church attendance and just knowing about God. They focus on their efforts and shortcomings, which hinders their ability to experience God to the fullest. I want to tell you, you are loved, accepted, forgiven and embraced by God. You are designed and suited to *hear* His voice and *share* His voice. Christ's power and love are yours to experience and yours to give away.

The love and power of Jesus is to be demonstrated. Faith thinks, faith speaks and faith acts! Go and *be* the love and power of Jesus that you and this world so desperately need! Always remember Jesus *loves* you, the Father *knows* you and the Holy Spirit is *in* you! Now go out and *become* the *love* and *power* of God in your world!

THE **NON-NEGOTIABLES**

- Healing is *always* the will of God and should be released by His active Church on the earth.
- Wisdom, practical awareness and *love* go a long way in praying for those with various ailments.
- Prophecy and words of knowledge are accessible to all believers. They radically mark those who receive the words as well as those who give them by releasing the Kingdom of God into their lives.
- We are not meant to be reservoirs, collecting the voice of God, but *rivers* who are willing to give it away also.

REFLECTION QUESTIONS

Jesus came to destroy the works of the devil, sickness and disease included. (See page 262.) Pray, Ask and Listen: Are there people in your life in need of God's healing touch? Write their names and pray for them. When an opportunity presents itself, call them or meet with them to pray for healing. Always remember the Word of God and Prayer are seeds and will eventually produce fruit when properly cultivated. Document the experience in the space provided.

_____
_____
_____
_____
_____

Words of knowledge provide information about a person that *only* God could know. (See page 292.) Have you seen these types of words given by you or by someone else? What is the impact of sharing these things with people? Why is it so important to use these gifts for New Testament evangelism?

___

Ministry is simply transferring the life force found in Jesus to others. (See page 315.) All believers are called to this ministry. Pray, Ask and Listen: Write out detailed goals as to how you can maximize your ministry of reconciliation, which is helping people to have a deeper connectedness and harmony with God. How will this in-depth study of God's voice impact this ministry?

ACTIVATION DECREE

I decree and declare that I am a vessel, fit for the service of the King. Each impartation I have gained through this book to hear God's voice will be used to enable me to share God's voice as well. From this moment forward, I decree, by faith, that my receptivity to the voice of God will be heightened in ways I have never before seen, in Jesus' mighty name, amen!

SETTING EXPECTATIONS

In the days, weeks and months to come, you should:

- Actively seek out opportunities to pray for those who are sick and hurting.
- Open yourself to the gifts of the Holy Spirit as you approach people in your daily interactions. Step out in faith and take risks!
- Practice sharing your testimony with family, friends and those you meet on the street, in your workplace or in your daily sphere of influence.
- Make the core value of your life to live in close communion with Jesus and extend the benefits of that relationship to the world around you *daily*.

Feel free to write out further goals, expectations and God encounters in the space below:

_____

_____

_____

_____
_____
_____
_____
_____
_____
_____
_____
_____
_____

Jesus loves you, and so do we!

Go out and become His love and His voice!

14

SPREADING GOD'S LOVE AND PARTNERSHIP

If this book has been a blessing to you we invite you to spread God's love by recommending it to your family, friends, Church, coworkers and loved ones. When God called me to write this book He said, *"I want My people to hear My voice I want you to give this book away freely so that My people may know Me better."* Keeping to the spirit of what God said to me, we have offered this book free of charge for anyone who cannot afford one postage paid on us. We don't want anyone to go without a book who wants one. So if you or someone you know needs additional copies of this book and for whatever reason cannot afford to purchase it please email us. Our heart is to get this book into the hands, and more importantly into the hearts, of as many people as possible.

We also would like to encourage you to prayerfully consider partnering with us financially, so we can spread these books and the Gospel message of an intimate relationship with God all over the world! The truth that God is alive, He speaks, everyone can hear His voice and experience His presence! Just talk to God about what He might potentially like you to give into our ministry either for a monthly contribution or a one-time gift. Whatever God puts on your heart to give would be a blessing to us even if it's just $5 a month. No matter if God moves you to give into our ministry or not, we pray that this book and our ministry resources have been and will be a blessing to you and your family for years to come!

GIVING

Your generosity enables Sterling Harris as well as the Sterling Harris Ministries Team to effectively minister the Gospel worldwide. Every available resource that God provides for this ministry is through the generosity of our Partners and Friends. Together, we are able to minister the good news of the Gospel to the world. Your donations will be used to teach and equip people with the message of salvation, faith, healing, freedom, intimacy, prosperity, and a vibrant relationship with God worldwide.

STERLINGHARRIS.ORG/DONATIONS

CHECKS CAN BE MAILED TO:

Sterling Harris Ministries
PO BOX 28
Jarrell, Texas 76537

You can send donations via PayPal using our scan code below by simply opening up the camera on your smartphone like you are going to take a picture of the barcode and your phone will prompt you to open up PayPal and take you right to our Ministries PayPal Page.

GIVING

Thank you for playing a vital role in this ministry of sharing Jesus with the world!

"Give, and it will be given to you. Good measure, pressed down, shaken together, running over, will be put into your lap. For with the measure you deal out [with the measure you use when you confer benefits on others, it will be measured back to you." Luke 6:38

AUTHOR BIO

Through the Word of God, Sterling's mission in life is to inspire people to reach higher; by starting and developing an intimate love relationship with Jesus Christ that is real, personal and powerful, led by the Holy Spirit. That powerful relationship will enable anyone who abides in the Word and lives in close communication with the Father to overcome any of life's circumstances and all adversity. His passion is helping fellow human beings experience God's love, power and presence.

Sterling's goal is to illustrate how through a love relationship with Jesus Christ and by putting the Word of God first place in our lives, we can all empower each other to achieve true success and prosperity. God promises in His Word that a prosperous life in Him will be whole, healed, free, and victorious! Sterling wants to inspire other people to reach their true potential and God's Best by teaching them how to operate their Faith at Christ Kingdom Levels. Thus, causing them to live out their intended purpose and calling; which is to model and demonstrate God's love and power to the whole world.

Sterling Harris was born in Dallas, TX and grew up in Terrell, TX. Sterling was a high school football standout with an array of awards including Super-Prep All-American, All-State, All-Area, and All-District, as well as a top four finalist for Class 4A Player of the Year in the State of Texas. He also excelled in the classroom as an honor roll student, and he graduated in the top 10% of his class from Terrell High School. Sterling was voted "Best All Around Boy" his senior year. During this time, he also owned and operated his own company specializing in acreage mowing and commercial cleanup.

During his years at SMU, Sterling worked for a variety of companies that include Morgan Stanley Dean Witter, State Farm Insurance, Sewell Motor Companies, and ORIX Real Estate Capital Markets where he refined his business skills. Sterling holds a Business Management degree from the Cox School of Business at Southern Methodist University. While attending SMU, he was a four-year football letterman at the right tackle position. After graduation, he signed an NFL contract with the Cleveland Browns. Sterling suffered a broken foot during his rookie season. After battling back from the injury, the Browns sent him to NFL Europe where he played and started at the offensive tackle position for the Frankfurt Galaxy. Sterling was forced into early retirement by a recurring foot injury he suffered in NFL Europe after his second year in the NFL.

Through this difficulty and other challenges Sterling learned how to overcome adversity by seeking God's Word, presence, Spirit and will for his life, even in the midst of great hardships. As he sought the Lord, he realized it is how you respond in faith to challenges that determine your true success in life. Through surrendering to God's will and eventually God's calling on his life into the Ministry, he has stayed God-motivated, and he has been able to live as an overcomer. Sterling has always had a giving spirit, and his spirit really bloomed as the Father began to teach him how to have a spiritual love relationship with Jesus Christ empowered by the Holy Spirit. Experiencing the heavenly Father's love has transformed Sterling into the free and giving man of God living in a love relationship with Jesus Christ and being led by the Holy Spirit, that he is today.

Sterling also spreads the Love of Christ through motivational speaking with his adopted brother Devonric Johnson.

Sterling is happily married to his wife Leah and they have a beautiful daughter named Gracie with more to follow if the Lord says the same. They also have two lovable dogs.

God Bless YOU! And remember this always, Jesus loves YOU!

#SpreadGodsLove

SOCIAL LINKS:

facebook.com/sterlingharris.org
twitter.com/shministries75
instagram.com/sterlingharrisministries
youtube.com/sterlingharrisministries

www.ingramcontent.com/pod-product-compliance
Lightning Source LLC
Chambersburg PA
CBHW071326080526
44587CB00018B/3359